BTEC Level 2 First Study Skills Guide in IT

Welcome to your Study Skills Guide! You can make it your own – start by adding your personal and course details below...

Learner's name: _____

BTEC course title: _____

Date started: _____

Mandatory units:

_____

_____

_____

Optional units:

_____

_____

_____

_____

Centre name: _____

Centre address:

_____

_____

_____

Tutor's name: _____

Published by Pearson Education Limited, a company incorporated in England and Wales, having its registered office at Edinburgh Gate, Harlow, Essex, CM20 2JE. Registered company number: 872828

Edexcel is a registered trademark of Edexcel Limited

Text © Pearson Education Limited 2010

First published 2010

13 12 11 10

10 9 8 7 6 5 4 3 2 1

British Library Cataloguing in Publication Data
A catalogue record for this book is available from the British Library

ISBN 978 1 84690 570 4

Typeset and edited by Ken Vail Graphic Design
Cover design by Visual Philosophy, created by eMC Design
Cover photo/illustration © Shutterstock: Yuri Arcurs
Printed in Slovakia by Neografia

Acknowledgements
The publisher would like to thank Microsoft for Microsoft product screenshots on pages 50–1, reprinted with permission from Microsoft Corporation.

Picture Credits
The publisher would like to thank the following for their kind permission to reproduce their photographs:

Alamy Images: Bob Johns / expresspictures.co.uk 11, Ace Stock Limited 55, Jacky Chapman, Janine Wiedel Photolibrary 15; **Corbis**: 62, Comstock 5; **iStockphoto**: 40; **Pearson Education Ltd**: Steve Shott 24, Ian Wedgewood 34; **Pearson Education Ltd**: Rob Judges 36; **TopFoto**: John Powell 20

Cover images: *Front*: **Shutterstock**: Yuri Arcurs

All other images © Pearson Education

Every effort has been made to trace the copyright holders and we apologise in advance for any unintentional omissions. We would be pleased to insert the appropriate acknowledgement in any subsequent edition of this publication.

Websites
Go to www.pearsonhotlinks.co.uk to gain access to the relevant website links and information on how they can aid your studies. When you access the site, search for either the title BTEC Level 2 First Study Skills Guide in IT or ISBN 9781846905704.

Disclaimer
This material has been published on behalf of Edexcel and offers high-quality support for the delivery of Edexcel qualifications.
This does not mean that the material is essential to achieve any Edexcel qualification, nor does it mean that it is the only suitable material available to support any Edexcel qualification. Edexcel material will not be used verbatim in setting any Edexcel examination or assessment. Any resource lists produced by Edexcel shall include this and other appropriate resources.
Copies of official specifications for all Edexcel qualifications may be found on the Edexcel website: www.edexcel.com

Contents

Popular progression pathways

General qualification	Vocationally related qualification	Applied qualification
Undergraduate Degree	BTEC Higher National	Foundation Degree
GCE AS and A level	BTEC National	Advanced Diploma
GCSE	BTEC First	Higher (L2) and Foundation (L1) Diplomas

Your BTEC First course
Early days

Every year many new learners start BTEC Level 2 First courses, enjoy the challenge and successfully achieve their award. Some do this the easy way; others make it harder for themselves.

Everyone will have different feelings when they start their course.

Case study: Positive thinking

Rashad and Alice are two new friends you have met on the BTEC Level 2 First. They have each sent you an email, as shown below:

From: Rashad
I don't really understand half the stuff on this course and I don't like that teacher we got for Unit 6. Anyway, I'm not going to get stressed over it – if it goes on like this I will probably drop out.

From: Alice
I'm finding the course quite confusing – with the different units and lots of new stuff – but I'm going to try really hard to get it all sorted out as I need to get a good grade at the end. I like most of the teachers. That Unit 6 one is a bit miserable, but I'm not going to let that put me off.

Which of their attitudes do you think most closely resembles your own? What is the best approach to dealing with things you don't understand or don't like on the course?

We all have times when we don't feel motivated, either by the course we are taking or by life in general. This can be for all sorts of reasons. Think of three ways of dealing with feeling negative or demotivated about some aspect of the course. For example, maybe you could chat with your friends about it.

You might find it helpful to prepare for these times by writing down why you want to do the course, the things you like about it and how it will help you with your future plans. When you feel demotivated, use these notes to remind yourself why you are doing the course.

About your course

What do you know already?

If someone asks you about your course, could you give a short, accurate description? If you can, you have a good understanding of what your course is about. This has several benefits.

TOP TIP

If you have a part-time job, you're likely to be involved in helping customers and colleagues. These are important skills for any BTEC First learner.

Four benefits of understanding your course

1. You will be better prepared and organised.
2. You can make links between the course and the world around you.
3. You can check how your personal interests and hobbies relate to the course.
4. You will be alert to information that relates to topics you are studying, whether it's from conversations with family and friends, watching television or at a part-time job.

TRY THIS

Write down your interests and hobbies and identify those that relate to your studies in any way.

Read any information you have been given by your centre. You can also check the Edexcel website for further details – go to www.edexcel.com

Interest/hobby	How this relates to my studies

What else do you need to know?

Five facts you should find out about your course

1. The type of BTEC qualification you are studying.
2. How many credits your qualification is worth.
3. The number of core units you will study and what they cover.
4. How many credits the mandatory units are worth.
5. The number of specialist units you need to study in total and the options available in your centre.

Case study: How will this course be useful?

Tony is a big football fan. He has discovered that he can use his interest in football to help him practise his IT skills. He has created a 'fanzine' (a magazine for football fans) to practise his desktop publishing skills and also produces a newsletter which is actually sent out to his 5-a-side football club members. He has created an Excel spreadsheet which lists data on all the first team members of the Premier League team he supports. The spreadsheet shows how many matches each player has played, how many goals they have scored and lots of other information and statistics. He is now thinking about producing a supporter's website.

Tony works part-time in a sports shop and has also created a spreadsheet to keep track of the hours he works. Recently, he was underpaid so he took the spreadsheet to his manager to show him the mistake. His manager was so impressed that he asked Tony to produce a spreadsheet that could be used to keep track of all temporary staff hours.

Tony is an excellent example of someone who has used his interests and part-time work to help develop his IT skills. This can be very useful when you apply for a job, as most employers like to see how you can relate what you have learnt on a course to their business.

Think about your interests, and any part-time or voluntary work that you do. How could you use IT to assist you in these areas?

BTEC FACT

BTEC First Certificate = 15 credits

BTEC First Extended Certificate = 30 credits

BTEC First Diploma = 60 credits

Generally, the more credits there are, the longer it takes to study for the qualification.

TRY THIS

Find out which optional units your centre offers. To check the topics covered in each unit go to www.edexcel.com and search for your qualification.

TOP TIP

If you have a choice of optional units in your centre and are struggling to decide, talk through your ideas with your tutor.

Activity: How well do you know your course?

Complete this activity to check that you know the main facts. Compare your answers with a friend. You should have similar answers except where you make personal choices, such as about optional units. Your tutor can help you complete number 9.

1 The correct title of the BTEC award I am studying is:

_____

_____

2 The length of time it will take me to complete my award is:

_____

_____

3 The number of mandatory units I have to study is:

_____

_____

4 The titles of my mandatory units, and their credit values, are:

_____

_____

_____

_____

_____

_____

_____

_____

_____

_____

5 The main topics I will learn in each mandatory unit include:

Mandatory unit	Main topics

6 The number of credits I need to achieve by studying optional units is:

7 The titles of my optional units, and their credit values, are:

8 The main topics I will learn in each optional unit include:

Optional unit	Main topics

9 Other important aspects of my course are:

_____

_____

_____

_____

10 After I have achieved my BTEC First, my options include:

_____

_____

_____

_____

_____

_____

Introduction to the information technology sector

BTEC Level 2 First in IT is a qualification for anyone who wants to develop IT application skills. These skills will help you in your future career to create documents, communicate and find information. The qualification covers a wide range of applications through the many optional units, focusing on word processing, databases, graphics, web page creation, and more. These skills are relevant to a very wide range of careers. Today, most careers require IT skills and it may be that you are studying on this course to complement a main area of study such as business studies, graphic design or many other areas.

Most careers today require IT skills.

For most businesses, information technology is a tool – like effective staff and efficient use of resources – to help them achieve their goals. They don't, for example, use spreadsheets for fun or have the latest model of computer because they look good. Like all business tools, information technology must therefore earn its keep; it must be able to help the business run efficiently and carry out the required tasks quickly and accurately. Successfully achieving these aims is largely down to the skills of the user – that's you! If you can't get the computer system to do what is required then an expensive business tool is a wasted resource.

What units will you be studying? You should have made a list of these in the previous section.

For more information about what you need to learn for each unit, look in the Unit Content section in the specification. Then complete the skills survey table below.

After filling in the unit name, look at the 'How familiar I am with this topic' column. Enter a number between 1 and 10, where 1 means you know nothing about the topic and 10 means you are very familiar with every aspect of the topic. Then complete the other two columns.

Unit name	How familiar I am with this topic (1–10)	Things I already know (check Unit Content in the specification)	Things I need to learn (check Unit Content in the specification)

Case study: Introduction to your sector

Simon completed his BTEC Level 2 First in ICT User in 2007. He now works as a Junior IT Support Technician in a hospital. After he completed his BTEC First, he went on to study for a BTEC National focusing on Networking and IT Support.

'The BTEC First provided a good introduction to the IT sector. We did quite a lot of different units and this helped me realise that some areas, such as software development, were not for me, but others, such as IT support, were. The work experience we did was also very useful and that, along with the work experience we did on the BTEC National, was very helpful in enabling me to get a job. Employers were also keen on that fact that I had done quite a lot of practical tasks on the course and not just theory. We also did several visits to companies to see what working as an IT professional involved. To be honest, I was quite surprised how much technical knowledge is required and also how highly employers rate non-technical skills such as customer service and communication skills.

'I enjoy the job I am doing now and get to use many of the skills I learnt on my BTEC First course, although I still have a lot to learn. I'm only a junior technician so sometimes I get the boring and repetitive jobs to do, but there are plenty of opportunities to progress. I want to specialise in networking and my current employer has said they will send me on some specialist courses that I need in order to develop my skills. In this industry you need to specialise to get the more interesting and better paid jobs.

'Looking back, I think the BTEC First gave me a really good start in the IT industry and taught me valuable skills that I have been building on ever since.'

Think about the kind of career you would like your BTEC course to lead to.

Skills you need for your sector

What skills does an employer expect from someone with an IT User qualification? Obviously, IT skills are essential! You should be proficient at using a computer and have excellent skills in the most commonly used applications, such as a word processor, spreadsheet software, email and the Internet, and in a number of specialist applications, such as database or web page creation software.

The following is a list of general IT skills and competencies you would be expected to have.

- **Keyboarding skills**
  You will be expected to have reasonable keyboard skills and be able to type quickly and accurately. You won't necessarily need to be able to touch type, although this is a very useful skill you should consider learning.

Do you know what touch typing is? If not, find out! Is there any software available to help you learn this skill?

- **Save, find and retrieve files and keep files safe**

  As well as understanding the basics, in a work environment you will be expected to keep track of a large number of important files and be able to find any one of them quickly.

  How can you keep your coursework in a way that makes finding any file easy? What precautions should you take to ensure you don't lose any work?

- **General IT housekeeping and problem solving**

  While you won't be expected to be a technical expert, you should know how to keep your computer running efficiently and how to deal with minor problems.

- **Security issues**

  Keeping your computer safe and secure is very important. You will be expected to know how to keep documents secure. This will be more important if you work in an area where you deal with confidential or personal information. You will be expected to understand your responsibilities under the Data Protection Act and to know what sensible precautions you should take to protect the computer system from viruses and hackers.

- **Internet and email skills**

  These are essential tools in a contemporary business so you will be expected to be fully proficient in the business use of these tools.

Activity: Gaining IT skills

Ashwin is interested in running his own business, but he is not yet sure exactly what that business will be. He is studying BTEC Level 2 First in Business but is also studying BTEC Level 2 First in IT as he knows IT skills are essential for anyone who wants to run their own business.

Ashwin is working on the following units:

- Unit 4: Business IT Skills
- Unit 6: Project Planning using IT
- Unit 16: Database Systems
- Unit 22: Doing Business Online
- Unit 36: Spreadsheet Modelling
- Unit 34: Website Production.

For each unit, think about how the skills Ashwin will learn might be relevant to his plans to start his own business. For example, how would project planning skills help Ashwin set up his new business?

Use the table below to list how each unit could be used.

Unit	How skills learnt could be used by Ashwin when he starts his business
Unit 4: Business IT Skills	
Unit 6: Project Planning using IT	
Unit 16: Database Systems	
Unit 22: Doing Business Online	
Unit 36: Spreadsheet Modelling	
Unit 34: Website Production	

What plans do you have for the future? How are the units you are studying relevant to those plans?

Your BTEC course will help you develop all-round skills, like communication.

More about BTEC First

What is different about a BTEC First?

How you learn

Expect to be 'hands-on'. BTEC Firsts are practical and focus on the skills and knowledge needed in the workplace. You will learn new things, and learn how to apply your knowledge.

BTEC First learners are expected to take responsibility for their own learning and be keen and well-organised. You should enjoy having more freedom, while knowing you can still ask for help or support if you need it.

How you are assessed

Many BTEC First courses are completed in one year, but if you are taking GCSEs as well, you may be doing it over two years or more. You will be assessed by completing **assignments** written by your tutors. These are based on **learning outcomes** set by Edexcel. Each assignment will have a deadline.

TOP TIP

Doing your best in assignments involves several skills, including managing your time so that you don't get behind. See pages 23–26 for tips on managing your time more efficiently.

BTEC FACT

On a BTEC course you achieve individual criteria at Pass, Merit or Distinction for your assignments. You will receive a Pass, Merit or Distinction **grade** for completed units and then one of these three grades for the whole course.

Case study: Completing assignments

At first, Alice found her BTEC course a bit strange. She left school after completing her GCSEs and decided to go to college to study BTEC Level 2 First in IT as she wanted to work in an office with computers.

At school she was used to a full timetable every day, so it was a bit of a surprise to find she only had lessons on four days each week – and even on the days when she was in college, there were some quite long gaps between lessons.

At first, she took the free time as time to relax, chat to her friends and go shopping. Her tutor had spoken to the class about using their time wisely but she hadn't taken much notice. When the first assignment was handed out she expected there would be enough time in the lessons to complete the work, but this didn't really happen and her teachers didn't give the class much time to do the assignment work in class.

As the deadline approached, she began to get worried as her work was nowhere near complete. When she had her monthly learning plan meeting with her tutor, she admitted to him that she was behind with her first assignment (which was due that week) and hadn't even started on her second one. Her tutor printed out a copy of her timetable and they agreed that she would work independently in the college Learning Resource Centre for three separate hour-long sessions each week. They pencilled these on her timetable. Her tutor also put Alice in touch with one of the Learning Resource Centre advisors who could give her help and encouragement to stay on track with her assignment work.

Alice used these sessions to catch up and, although her first assignment was handed in late, she managed to get her second one completed on time. She soon got used to the more independent nature of the BTEC course and used her 'free' time wisely to work on assignments. After she had caught up with her work, she didn't need to use every session she had pencilled in on her timetable; she learned to be flexible, spending more time in the Learning Resource Centre as and when she needed to.

Getting the most from your BTEC

Getting the most from your BTEC involves several skills, such as using your time effectively and working well with other people. Knowing yourself is also important.

Knowing yourself

How would you describe yourself? Make some notes here.

_____

_____

_____

_____

_____

_____

_____

_____

If you described yourself to someone else, would you be able to sum up your temperament and personality, identify your strengths and weaknesses and list your skills? If not, is it because you've never thought about it or because you honestly don't have a clue?

Learning about yourself is often called self-analysis. You may have already done personality tests or careers profiles. If not, there are many available online. However, the information you gain from these profiles is useless unless you can apply it to what you are doing.

Your personality

Everyone is different. For example, some people:
- like to plan in advance; others prefer to be spontaneous
- love being part of a group; others prefer one or two close friends
- enjoy being the life and soul of the party; others prefer to sit quietly and feel uncomfortable at large social gatherings
- are imaginative and creative; others prefer to deal only with facts
- think carefully about all their options before making a decision; others follow their 'gut instincts' and often let their heart rule their head.

Case study: Your personality and the BTEC First

No two people are the same! Of course you know that, but it's important to be aware that different people have different strengths. This can affect not only the way that they study, but also the sort of job that they would be good at, and enjoy the most.

The following three learners are studying BTEC Level 2 First in IT:

Winston is a very outgoing person. He is friendly and likes to chat. He is sometimes a bit forgetful and he gets bored easily. Winston doesn't like the same routine every day.

Wendy is a quiet person who works best on her own. She is very good at detail and following instructions.

Aftab loves challenges and solving problems. He is good at explaining things but is not good at working on his own unsupervised.

Below is a list of jobs that each of these learners might consider doing when they finish the course:

- Web page developer – working at home developing web pages for clients
- IT applications trainer – travelling around the country delivering short training courses to business people
- IT application help desk operator – working in an office answering telephone calls from clients who have problems with their computers
- Administration assistant – working in an office using computer software to create reports, presentations and brochures.

Think about the people listed above. Which of them would be the most suitable for each job?

TRY THIS

Imagine one of your friends is describing your best features. What would they say?

Personalities in the workplace

There's a mix of personalities in most workplaces. Some people prefer to work behind the scenes, such as many IT practitioners, who like to concentrate on tasks they enjoy doing. Others love high-profile jobs, where they may often be involved in high-pressure situations, such as paramedics and television presenters. Most people fall somewhere between these two extremes.

In any job there will be some aspects that are more appealing and interesting than others. If you have a part-time job you will already know this. The same thing applies to any course you take!

Your personality and your BTEC First course

Understanding your personality means you can identify which parts of your course you are likely to find easy and which more difficult. Working out the aspects you need to develop should be positive. You can also think about how your strengths and weaknesses may affect other people.

- Natural planners find it easier to schedule work for assignments.
- Extroverts like giving presentations and working with others but may overwhelm quieter team members.
- Introverts often prefer to work alone and may be excellent at researching information.

> **BTEC FACT**
>
> All BTEC First courses enable you to develop your personal, learning and thinking skills (**PLTS**), which will help you to meet new challenges more easily. (See page 81.)

Activity: What is your personality type?

1a) Identify your own personality type, either by referring to a personality test you have done recently or by going online and doing a reliable test. Go to page 90 to find out how to access a useful website for this activity.

Print a summary of the completed test or write a brief description of the results for future reference.

b) Use this information to identify the tasks and personal characteristics that you find easy or difficult.

	Easy	Difficult
Being punctual		
Planning how to do a job		
Working neatly and accurately		
Being well organised		
Having good ideas		
Taking on new challenges		
Being observant		
Working with details		
Being patient		
Coping with criticism		
Dealing with customers		
Making decisions		
Keeping calm under stress		
Using your own initiative		

	Easy	Difficult
Researching facts carefully and accurately		
Solving problems		
Meeting deadlines		
Finding and correcting own errors		
Clearing up after yourself		
Helping other people		
Working as a member of a team		
Being sensitive to the needs of others		
Respecting other people's opinions		
Being tactful and discreet		
Being even-tempered		

2 Which thing from your 'difficult' list do you think you should work on improving first? Start by identifying the benefits you will gain. Then decide how to achieve your goal.

Your knowledge and skills

You already have a great deal of knowledge, as well as practical and personal skills gained at school, at home and at work (if you have a part-time job). Now you need to assess these to identify your strengths and weaknesses.

To do this accurately, try to identify evidence for your knowledge and skills. Obvious examples are:

- previous qualifications
- school reports
- occasions when you have demonstrated particular skills, such as communicating with customers or colleagues in a part-time job.

TOP TIP

The more you understand your own personality, the easier it is to build on your strengths and compensate for your weaknesses.

Part-time jobs give you knowledge and skills in a real work setting.

Activity: Check your skills

1 Score yourself from 1 to 5 for each of the skills in the table opposite.

   1 = I'm very good at this skill.

   2 = I'm good but could improve this skill.

   3 = This skill is only average and I know that I need to improve it.

   4 = I'm weak at this skill and must work hard to improve it.

   5 = I've never had the chance to develop this skill.

   Enter the score in the column headed 'Score A' and add today's date.

2 Look back at the units and topics you will be studying for your course – you entered them into the chart on pages 9–10. Use this to identify any additional skills that you know are important for your course and add them to the table. Then score yourself for these skills, too.

3 Identify the main skills you will need in order to be successful in your chosen career, and highlight them in the table.

   Go back and score yourself against each skill after three, six and nine months. That way you can monitor your progress and check where you need to take action to develop the most important skills you will need.

English and communication skills	Score A (today) Date:	Score B (after three months) Date:	Score C (after six months) Date:	Score D (after nine months) Date:
Reading and understanding different types of texts and information				
Speaking to other people face to face				
Speaking clearly on the telephone				
Listening carefully				
Writing clearly and concisely				
Presenting information in a logical order				
Summarising information				
Using correct punctuation and spelling				
Joining in a group discussion				
Expressing your own ideas and opinions appropriately				
Persuading other people to do something				
Making an oral presentation and presenting ideas clearly				
ICT skills	Score A (today) Date:	Score B (after three months) Date:	Score C (after six months) Date:	Score D (after nine months) Date:
Using ICT equipment correctly and safely				
Using a range of software				
Accurate keyboarding				
Proofreading				
Using the internet to find and select appropriate information				
Using ICT equipment to communicate and exchange information				
Producing professional documents which include tables and graphics				
Creating and interpreting spreadsheets				
Using PowerPoint				

Maths and numeracy skills	Score A (today) Date:	Score B (after three months) Date:	Score C (after six months) Date:	Score D (after nine months) Date:
Carrying out calculations (eg money, time, measurements, etc) in a work-related situation				
Estimating amounts				
Understanding and interpreting data in tables, graphs, diagrams and charts				
Comparing prices and identifying best value for money				
Solving routine and non-routine work-related numerical problems				

Case study: Your knowledge and skills

Clive has a part-time job as a store assistant in a supermarket. As with most jobs, there are parts he likes and parts he doesn't like. He enjoys being helpful to customers and chatting to them. He knows in which aisle just about any product you can think of can be found – he finds it an enjoyable challenge to remember where unusual items are located, and enjoys directing customers to them. He is happy stacking shelves with stock – even though it is monotonous, he doesn't mind. He likes the store when it is busy and there is a lot to do. He also enjoys supporting the checkout staff, rushing about finding things for customers and getting replacement items when the bar code is missing.

However, Clive doesn't get on well with his boss and doesn't like being told what to do and being pestering by him about things which aren't important. He also hates filling in forms and doing stock checks with the fiddly hand-held computer. He isn't very good at turning up on time, especially when he starts early as he finds it difficult to wake up.

What strengths and weaknesses do you think Clive has? What strengths and weaknesses do you have? Are any of them similar to Clive's? How do you think you (or Clive) could try to overcome these weaknesses?

Managing your time

Some people are brilliant at managing their time. They do everything they need to and have time left over for activities they enjoy. Other people complain that they don't know where the time goes.

Which are you? If you need help to manage your time – and most people do – you will find help here.

Why time management is important

- It means you stay in control, get less stressed and don't skip important tasks.
- Some weeks will be peaceful, others will be hectic.
- The amount of homework and assignments you have to do will vary.
- As deadlines approach, time always seems to go faster.
- Some work will need to be done quickly, maybe for the next lesson; other tasks may need to be done over several days or weeks. This needs careful planning.
- You may have several assignments or tasks to complete in a short space of time.
- You want to have a social life.

Avoiding time-wasting

We can all plan to do work, and then find our plans go wrong. There may be several reasons for this. How many of the following do *you* do?

Top time-wasting activities
1 Allowing (or encouraging) people to interrupt you.
2 Not having the information, handouts or textbook you need because you've lost them or lent them to someone else.
3 Chatting to people, making calls or sending texts when you should be working.
4 Getting distracted because you simply must keep checking out MySpace, Facebook or emails.
5 Putting off jobs until they are a total nightmare, then panicking.
6 Daydreaming.
7 Making a mess of something so you have to start all over again.

Planning and getting organised

The first step in managing your time is to plan ahead and be well organised. Some people are naturally good at this. They think ahead, write down their commitments in a diary or planner, and store their notes and handouts neatly and carefully so they can find them quickly.

How good are your working habits?

Improving your planning and organisational skills

1 Use a diary or planner to schedule working times into your weekdays and weekends.

2 Have a place for everything and everything in its place.

3 Be strict with yourself when you start work. If you aren't really in the mood, set a shorter time limit and give yourself a reward when the time is up.

4 Keep a diary in which you write down exactly what work you have to do.

5 Divide up long or complex tasks into manageable chunks and put each 'chunk' in your diary with a deadline of its own.

6 Write a 'to do' list if you have several different tasks. Tick them off as you go.

7 Always allow more time than you think you need for a task.

Talking to friends can take up a lot of time.

Case study: Avoiding time wasters

Ali has two assignments to hand in on Friday. He plans to do some work on them over the weekend then finish them off in class. Saturday is a busy day, but Ali foresees no problems as Sunday will be quiet. However, he stays up late on Saturday night, wakes up feeling lazy, and it's not until after 4 pm on Sunday that he thinks about doing some assignment work. He makes a good start, but TV and phone calls distract him and he doesn't get far.

Monday is a hectic day at college so he makes little progress. On the way home he has an argument with some boys from another school on the bus and ends up stressed and upset. He spends the evening chatting to his friends about it on MSN.

On Tuesday, Ali has a 2-hour IT lesson in the morning. However, the computer he uses in the class has some kind of problem and he cannot log on. By the time it gets fixed, the lesson is nearly over. When he gets home he starts up his PC and straight away a message pops up from his friend Andy. He spends the rest of the evening chatting and goes to bed at 1 am feeling guilty.

Ali doesn't have any IT lessons on Wednesday and in the evening he has football practice. He wakes up on Thursday in a panic. There are no IT lessons that day either, so he cannot make any further progress on the assignments at college. He gets home and works all evening and half the night on the assignments.

It's Friday morning and all Ali needs to do is make a few additions to his assignments and print them off. When he gets to his IT lesson, he plugs his USB memory stick into the computer and a box pops up saying, 'This device is not formatted. Do you want to format it now?' In a panic he checks with the IT technician, but he says the USB is faulty. Ali's heart sinks as the technician says, 'I hope you've got a backup …'.

Reflect on the mistakes that Ali made. For each mistake, think of a way you can avoid making the same mistake.

It can be very difficult to avoid getting distracted when working. Think of ways to help you stay focused when you are working.

TOP TIP

If you become distracted by social networking sites or email when you're working, set yourself a time limit of 10 minutes or so to indulge yourself.

BTEC FACT

If you have serious problems that are interfering with your ability to work or to concentrate, talk to your tutor. There are many ways in which BTEC learners who have personal difficulties can be supported to help them continue with their studies.

Activity: Managing time

1 The correct term for something you do in preference to starting a particular task is a 'displacement activity'. In the workplace this includes things like often going to the water cooler to get a drink, and constantly checking emails and so on online. People who work from home may tidy up, watch television or even cook a meal to put off starting a job.

Write down *your* top three displacement activities.

2 Today is Wednesday. Sajid has several jobs to do tonight and has started well by making a 'to do' list. He's worried that he won't get through all the things on his list and because he works on Thursday and Friday evenings that the rest will have to wait until Saturday.

a) Look through Sajid's list and decide which jobs are top priority and *must* be done tonight and which can be left until Saturday if he runs out of time.

b) Sajid is finding that his job is starting to interfere with his ability to do his assignments. What solutions can you suggest to help him?

Jobs to do

– File handouts from today's classes

– Phone Tom (left early today) to tell him the time of our presentation tomorrow has been changed to 11 am

– Research information online for next Tuesday's lesson

– Complete table from rough notes in class today

– Rewrite section of leaflet to talk about at tutorial tomorrow

– Write out class's ideas for the charity of the year, ready for course representatives meeting tomorrow lunchtime

– Redo handout Tom and I are giving out at presentation

– Plan how best to schedule assignment received today – deadline 3 weeks

– Download booklet from website ready for next Monday's class

---

TRY THIS ➡

Write down your current commitments and how long they take each week. Then decide those that are top priority and those that you could postpone in a very busy week.

Getting the most from work experience

On some BTEC First courses, all learners have to do a **work placement**. On others, they are recommended but not essential, or are required only for some optional units. If you are doing one, you need to prepare for it so that you get the most out of it. The checklists in this section will help.

Before you go checklist

1 Find out about the organisation by researching online.

2 Check that you have all the information you'll need about the placement.

3 Check the route you will need to take and how long it will take you. Always allow longer on the first day.

4 Check with your tutor what clothes are suitable and make sure you look the part.

5 Check that you know any rules or guidelines you must follow.

6 Check that you know what to do if you have a serious problem during the placement, such as being too ill to go to work.

7 Talk to your tutor if you have any special personal concerns.

8 Read the unit(s) that relate to your placement carefully. Highlight points you need to remember or refer to regularly.

9 Read the assessment criteria that relate to the unit(s) and use these to make a list of the information and evidence you'll need to obtain.

10 Your tutor will give you an official logbook or diary – or just use a notebook. Make notes each evening while things are fresh in your mind, and keep them safely.

While you're on work placement

Ideally, on your first day you'll be told about the company and what you'll be expected to do. You may even be allocated to one particular member of staff who will be your 'mentor'. However, not all organisations operate like this and if everyone is very busy, your **induction** may be rushed. If so, stay positive and watch other people to see what they're doing. Then offer to help where you can.

BTEC FACT

If you need specific evidence from a work placement for a particular unit, your tutor may give you a logbook or work diary, and will tell you how you will be assessed in relation to the work that you will do.

TRY THIS

You're on work experience. The placement is interesting and related to the job you want to do. However, you've been watching people most of the time and want to get more involved. Identify three jobs you think you could offer to do.

While you're there

1 Arrive with a positive attitude, knowing that you are going to do your best and get the most out of your time there.

2 Although you may be nervous at first, don't let that stop you from smiling at people, saying 'hello' and telling them your name.

3 Arrive punctually – or even early – every day. If you're delayed for any reason, phone and explain. Then get there as soon as you can.

4 If you take your mobile phone, switch it off when you arrive.

5 If you have nothing to do, offer to help someone who is busy or ask if you can watch someone who is doing a job that interests you.

6 Always remember to thank people who give you information, show you something or agree that you can observe them.

7 If you're asked to do something and don't understand what to do, ask for it to be repeated. If it's complicated, write it down.

8 If a task is difficult, start it and then check back that you are doing it correctly before you go any further.

9 Obey all company rules, such as regulations and procedures relating to health and safety and using machinery, the use of IT equipment and access to confidential information.

10 Don't rush off as fast as you can at the end of the day. Check first with your mentor or supervisor whether you can leave.

Coping with problems

Problems are rare but can happen. The most common ones are being bored because you're not given any work to do or upset because you feel someone is treating you unfairly. Normally, the best first step is to talk to your mentor at work or your supervisor. However, if you're very worried or upset, you may prefer to get in touch with your tutor instead – do it promptly.

TOP TIP

Observing people who are skilled at what they do helps you learn a lot, and may even be part of your **assignment brief.**

Getting experience of work in IT

Case study: Steve's work experience

Steve has his work experience arranged at Turner's, a local estate agent in a town near his home. He was due there at 9:30 am, but had problems finding the office as he has forgotten to bring the folder of information he was given by his tutor. When he finally finds Turner's, the time is nearly 10 am. He walks in and the receptionist asks him, 'Can I help you?' Steve mumbles, 'Er, well, yes, I …' frantically trying to remember the name of the person he is supposed to ask for. 'I'm on work experience,' he eventually says.

The receptionist clearly does not know about this but eventually she works out that Mr Burrows, the office manager, is expecting Steve. 'Oh dear,' she says. 'You just missed him. He has gone to a meeting. I guess you can wait here until he gets back.' Steve sits embarrassed and bored for the best part of an hour in reception waiting for Mr Burrows. When he finally arrives, he is quite nice. 'I'm sorry,' he says. 'I had to go to the meeting. I thought you were coming at 9:30 and I would have time to show you around.' The rest of the morning goes quite well. Mr Burrows is friendly and so are the rest of the staff, although they all seem very busy.

After the lunch break, Mr Burrows asks Steve if he can do a word-processing mail merge. Steve remembers this vaguely so he says he can. Mr Burrows shows him various files on the PC and explains what to do, but Steve doesn't really understand any of it and has not got a pen or paper to write it down. Mr Burrows then goes out to another meeting. Steve sits at the computer and tries various things to get the mail merge done but he can't work it out. Everyone looks busy so he just pretends to be working.

Two hours later, Mr Burrows returns. 'Done the mail merge?' he asks. Steve is really embarrassed and apologises. Mr Burrows is reasonably understanding. As he leaves, Mr Burrows says to Steve quietly, 'We all dress fairly smart in the office, so you need to wear something a bit smarter tomorrow, with a tie.' Steve goes home feeling really demoralised.

Reflect on Steve's day. What could he have done to improve his work experience?

Activity: Work experience

Imagine that a really good work experience opportunity has come up at short notice and your tutor says that you start on Monday. Make a list of the things you would need to do and find out so you are fully prepared to start on Monday.

Things I need to do or find out before my work experience:

1

2

3

4

5

Use this as a check list when you start your work experience.

Finding work experience in the IT sector

Finding the right work experience placement can be difficult, but is very much worth the effort. Because IT is used in almost every industry, you can potentially find placements in all sorts of organisations. Generally you will have more success with larger organisations, as small companies may not have a dedicated IT department.

Often you will have more success finding work experience in the following types of organisations:

- schools
- colleges
- your local council
- voluntary organisations.

Make a list of the schools, colleges and voluntary organisations in your local area. You can find this information on the internet (your local council website should have a list of all the schools and colleges in your area).

Organisation	Telephone number	Email address

When you telephone an organisation to ask if they can take you on work experience, it is important to ask the right questions. Make the most of the conversation by having a 'script' to follow when you phone them. In the space below, draft a script to use when calling organisations. You need to ask to speak to the IT department, say what it is you want to do, when and for how long.

You may find that the employers interested in offering you work experience want to know what subjects you are doing on your course, and what sort of thing you would like to do or can do. Make a list of the tasks you can do, or would be interested in doing.

Working with other people

Everyone finds it easy to work with people they like and far harder with those they don't. On your course you'll often be expected to work as a team to do a task. This gives you practice in working with different people.

You will be expected to:

- contribute to the task
- listen to other people's views
- adapt to other people's ways of working
- take responsibility for your own contribution
- agree the best way to resolve any problems.

These are quite complex skills. It helps if you understand the benefits to be gained by working cooperatively with other people and know the best way to achieve this.

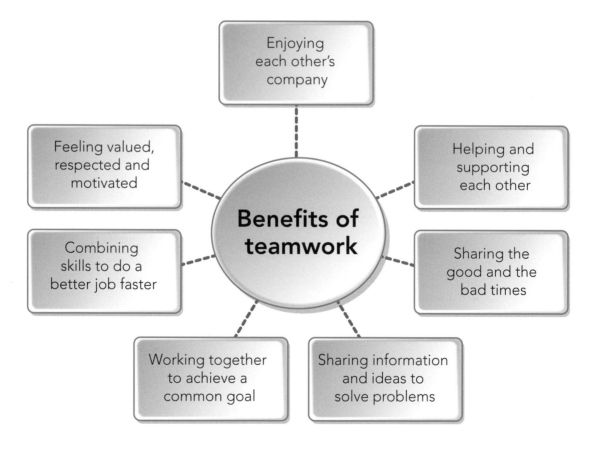

Benefits of teamwork

Golden rules for everyone (including the team leader!)

The secret of a successful team is that everyone works together. The role of the team leader is to make this as easy as possible by listening to people's views and coordinating everyone's efforts. A team leader is not there to give orders.

Positive teamwork checklist

✔ Be loyal to your team, including the team leader.

✔ Be reliable and dependable at all times.

✔ Be polite. Remember to say 'please' and 'thank you'.

✔ Think before you speak.

✔ Treat everyone the same.

✔ Make allowances for individual personalities. Give people 'space' if they need it, but be ready to offer support if they ask for it.

✔ Admit mistakes and apologise if you've done something wrong – learn from it but don't dwell on it.

✔ Give praise when it's due, give help when you can and thank people who help you.

✔ Keep confidences, and any promises that you make.

Do you:

a) shrug and say nothing in case he gets upset

b) ask why he didn't text you to give you warning

c) say that it's the last time you'll ever go anywhere with him and walk off?

Which do you think would be the most effective – and why?

TOP TIP

Being a good team member means putting the group's needs before your own.

TRY THIS

Work out whether you're usually passive, assertive or aggressive when you're annoyed. You've arranged to meet Sam to see a film. He arrives 20 minutes late.

Case study: Working as a team

The IT class at Northway School are completing an assignment for the Desktop Publishing unit – working in a team to design and produce a poster. Teamwork is a feature of real business life, so the assignment is good preparation for the world of work. The tutor splits the class into groups of three or four learners, but leaves each group to decide on the team leader and on how the different tasks will be allocated. Most of the groups work well, but three groups have problems.

- The learners in Group 1 argue constantly. They cannot agree on a group leader or on how to allocate the tasks.
- All the work in Group 2 is done by just one person and the other two learners do virtually nothing.
- Group 3 doesn't really work as a team: there is a group leader, but everyone does their own work and the group hardly ever meets.

Some members of the class feel that the teams would have worked better if the learners had chosen who would be in each group, as friends would work better together. The way the tutor has set up the groups puts friends apart from each other. The tutor points out that at work you cannot choose to work with friends, you have to be able to work with all sorts of people.

Think about the possible reasons why there were problems in the three groups above. How can you help to avoid these kinds of problems when working in a group?

There are many benefits to be gained from working as a team.

IT provides a number of ways in which people can work together without being physically in the same place. Teamwork using electronic communication methods is a very important skill, and it is likely that businesses will rely even more heavily on these methods in the future. You will probably already have used facilities such as email and Instant Messenger to chat to your friends. These, and other IT tools, are widely used in business to support teamwork, although obviously the communications are much more professional than those that take place between friends.

Activity: Email teamworking activity

This activity is designed to help you develop your electronic teamworking skills. You will need to find a group of three or four classmates who can work together on this. Your task is to arrange a meeting to discuss the group's opinions of the course (eg what you think of each of the units, how difficult it is, what you would like to see improved, etc). The meeting must be arranged entirely electronically, using email. You are required to do the following (all by email only):

- appoint a team leader
- agree a meeting time and place
- make suggestions about what should be discussed
- agree an agenda for the meeting.

When you have completed the task, hold a meeting with your group, either in person or using an instant message or chat session and discuss the following points.

- Was it easier or harder to carry out the task by email than it would have been in person? Give reasons.

What are the advantages of using email for this kind of activity? Remember that in a business context people may work from different locations.

Getting the most from special events

BTEC First courses usually include several practical activities and special events. These enable you to find out information, develop your skills and knowledge in new situations and enjoy new experiences. They may include visits to external venues, visits from specialist speakers, and team events.

Your tutor may be able to arrange a visit to a local business to learn how it uses IT to improve its business operations.

Most learners enjoy the chance to do something different. You'll probably look forward to some events more than others. If you're ready to get actively involved, you'll usually gain the most benefit. It also helps to make a few preparations!

Case study: Guest speakers

The course leader for the BTEC Level 2 First in IT arranges for two former learners to talk to the current class about their experiences of the course and how they have progressed since they finished. **Martin**, completed the course last year and is now studying for a BTEC National in IT. **Smita**, completed the course a couple of years ago and now has a job.

Martin explains how useful the BTEC Level 2 First in IT was for studying the Level 3 course – but he also says that Level 3 is quite a bit harder, especially when it comes to getting the higher grades. He encourages the learners to work hard to develop their skills and to try their best to get the higher grades as this will prepare them well for study at Level 3.

Smita has a job in a solicitor's office as an administrative assistant. She talks through the elements of the course she found most useful, such as work experience and developing skills

like research, independent learning and working with other people. She also explains that work can be very demanding and that she is expected to have excellent skills in a wide range of software and to produce complex documents quickly and accurately. When there are problems with the software or computer hardware, or she needs to do something she has not done before, there is often no-one she can turn to for help, so she has to be able to research procedures and fix problems herself. In fact, other people in the office often come to her with problems. At times, the pressure of work is quite high so she encourages the learners to develop good time management skills and to prepare for the world of work by keeping to deadlines.

What questions would you ask Martin or Smita?

Ask your tutor if it is possible for some former learners from the course to talk to your group.

Special events checklist

✔ Check you understand how the event relates to your course.

✔ If a visit or trip is not something you would normally find very interesting, try to keep an open mind. You might get a surprise!

✔ Find out what you're expected to do, and any rules or guidelines you must follow, including about your clothes or appearance.

✔ Always allow enough time to arrive five minutes early, and make sure you're never late.

✔ On an external visit, make notes on what you see and hear. This is essential if you have to write about it afterwards, use your information to answer questions in an assignment or do something practical.

✔ If an external speaker is going to talk to your class, prepare a list of questions in advance. Nominate someone to thank the speaker afterwards. If you want to record the talk, it's polite to ask first.

✔ For a team event, you may be involved in planning and helping to allocate different team roles. You'll be expected to participate positively in any discussions, to talk for some (but not all) of the time, and perhaps to volunteer for some jobs yourself.

✔ Write up any notes you make as soon as you can – while you can still understand what you wrote!

TRY THIS

At the last minute, you're asked to propose a vote of thanks to a visiting speaker on behalf of your class. What would you say?

Activity: Visiting an office

You get an email from your friend Rashad:

Hi!

You heard the news? We're going on a trip next Wednesday to a solicitor's office to see how they use IT. We will miss the IT lesson in the morning, which is a bit of a disappointment 'cos I like that lesson. I'm getting really good at using desktop publishing. I don't know why we have to go on a trip. Sounds really boring to me. I hope we're not supposed to ask any questions, I would have no idea what to ask. What do they do in a solicitor's office anyway? Maybe I'll just stay at the back or take a day off sick.

CU!

Rashad

It sounds like Rashad isn't looking forward to the trip. Write a reply to his email that will encourage him to look forward to it. Suggest ways in which he can usefully prepare for the office visit.

Resources and research

Understanding resources

Resources are items that help you do something. The most obvious one is money! To obtain your BTEC First award, however, your resources are rather different.

Physical resources

Physical resources are things like textbooks, computers and any specialist equipment.

- Popular textbooks, laptops for home use and specialist equipment may need to be booked. Leaving it until the last minute is risky.
- You can ask for help if you don't know how to use resources properly.
- You should check what stationery and equipment you need at the start of your course and make sure you have it.
- You need to look after your resources carefully. This saves money and time spent replacing lost items.

People as resources

There are many people who can help you through your course:

- family members who help and support you
- your tutor
- friends in your group who collect handouts for you and phone you to keep you up-to-date when you're absent
- librarians and computer technicians, at your centre or your local library
- expert practitioners.

Expert practitioners

Expert practitioners have worked hard to be successful in their chosen area. They know the skills and knowledge needed to do the job properly. They can be invaluable when you're researching information (see page 44). You can also learn a lot by watching them at work, especially if you can ask them questions about what they do, what they find hard and any difficulties they've had.

For businesses to operate efficiently, they need expert IT technicians who are able to diagnose and solve problems quickly.

Try to observe more than one expert practitioner:

- It gives you a better picture about what they do.
- No single job will cover all aspects of work that might apply to your studies.
- You may find some experts more approachable and easy to understand than others. For example, if someone is impatient because they're busy it may be difficult to ask them questions, or if someone works very quickly you may find it hard to follow what they're doing.

If you have problems, just note what you've learned and compare it with your other observations. And there's always the chance that you're observing someone who's not very good at their job! You'll only know this for certain if you've seen what people *should* be doing.

Activity: Creating a resource list

What other resources will you need for this course?

Clearly, access to a computer will be important! You will have access to computers for your practical classes, but what about outside class time? Having a computer at home is obviously beneficial. However, you might not have one, or you might need to share one with other family members. Your centre will provide access to computers in a library or learning resource centre, and your local public library may also have computers for public use.

You will need a USB memory stick ('pen' drive) to back up your work and transfer it between computers. It really is **absolutely essential** that you always keep a back up copy of your work. **Never** rely on a single copy. If you lose your work for whatever reason there is no alternative, you MUST do it again.

Make a list of the resources you will need to buy for the course (eg USB memory stick, folder, dividers, etc).

Books

You will need to think carefully about whether or not to buy IT books. As IT is a rapidly changing area, these books quickly become out of date. Research IT books via an online bookshop such as Amazon to make a list of suitable books.

Online tutorials

It is easy to find online tutorials for most of the common applications. For Microsoft Office, for example, you can use the excellent and comprehensive Office website (go to page 90 for details of how to access this website). The Office website contains many tutorials on Office applications – check out the 'Help' and 'How to' sections.

Magazines

There are many different computing magazines available at your local newsagents. Magazines are an excellent source of up-to-date information, but you'll need to select the right ones. Visit your local newsagents and look at the computing magazines available. Which ones might be useful for your course? Make a list of any suitable magazines that you find.

Finding the information you need

The information explosion

There are lots of different ways to find out information – books, newspapers, magazines, TV, radio, CDs, DVDs, the internet. And you can exchange information with other people by texting, sending an email or phoning someone.

All this makes it much easier to obtain information. If you know what you're doing, you can probably find most of what you need sitting at a computer. But there are some dangers:

- Finding exactly what you want online takes skill. You need to know what you're doing.
- It's easy to get too much information and become overwhelmed.
- It's unlikely that everything you need will be available online.
- The information you read may be out of date.
- The information may be neither reliable nor true.

Define what you are trying to find. (The more precise you are, the more likely you are to find what you're looking for.)

Know where to look for it. (Remember: the internet is not the only source of information.)

Recognise when you have found appropriate information.

Know what to do with information once you've found it. (Make sure that you understand it, interpret it correctly and record the source where you found it.)

Know when to stop looking (especially if you have a deadline).

Finding and using information effectively

Before you start

There are four things that will help you look in the right place and target your search properly.

Ask yourself ...	Because ...	Example
Exactly what do I need to find out?	It will save you time and effort.	If you need information about accidents, you need to know what type of accident and over what time period.
Why do I need this information and who is going to read it?	This puts the task into context. You need to identify the best type of information to obtain and how to get it.	If you're making a poster or leaflet for children, you'll need simple information that can be presented in a graphical format. If, however, you're giving a workplace presentation on accidents, you'll need tables and graphs to illustrate your talk.
Where can I find it?	You need to consider whether your source is trustworthy and up to date. The internet is great, but you must check that the sites you use are reliable.	To find out about accidents in the workplace you could talk to the health and safety at work officer. To find examples of accidents in your local area you could look through back copies of your local newspaper in the local library or newspaper offices.
What is my deadline?	You know how long you have to find the information and use it.	

TRY THIS

Schedule your research time by calculating backwards from the deadline date. Split the time you have 50/50 between searching for information and using it. This stops you searching for too long and getting lots of interesting material, but then not having the time to use it properly!

Your three main sources of information are libraries or learning resource centres, the internet, and other people, for example asking questions through interviews and questionnaires.

Researching in libraries

You can use the learning resource centre in your school or college, or a local public library. Public libraries usually have a large reference section with many resources available for loan, including CD-ROMs, encyclopaedias, government statistics, magazines, journals and newspapers, and databases such as Infotrac, which contains articles from newspapers and magazines over the last five years.

The librarian will show you how to find the resources you need and how to look up a specific book (or author) to check if it is available or is out on loan.

Some books and resources can only be used in the library itself, while others can be taken out on short-term or long-term loan. You need to plan how to access and use the resources that are popular or restricted.

Using your library

✔ If your centre has an intranet you might be able to check which books and CD-ROMs are available without actually visiting the library.

✔ All libraries have photocopying facilities, so take enough change with you to copy articles that you can't remove. Write down the source of any article you photocopy, ie the name and the date of the publication.

✔ Learn how to keep a reference file (or bibliography) in which you store the details of all your sources and references. A bibliography must include CDs, DVDs and other information formats, not just books and magazines.

✔ If your search is complicated, go at a quiet time when the librarian can help you.

✔ Don't get carried away if you find several books that contain the information you need. Too many can be confusing.

✔ Use the index to find information quickly by searching for key words. Scan the index using several likely alternatives.

✔ Only use books that you find easy to understand. A book is only helpful if you can retell the information in your own words.

TRY THIS

Search engines don't just find websites. On Google, the options at the top of your screen include 'images', 'news' and 'maps'. If you click on 'more' and then 'even more', you'll find other options, too. You'll usually find the most relevant information if you use the UK version of a search engine. Only search the whole web if you deliberately want to include European and American information.
Go to page 90 to find out how to see this in action.

Researching online

A good search engine such as Google will help you find useful websites. They look for sites based on the information you enter in the search box. In some cases, such as Ask.co.uk, you may get the chance to refine your choice after entering your key words or question.

Finding information on a website

Wikipedia is a popular free online encyclopaedia. It has been criticised because entries may be inaccurate as members of the public can edit the site. However, Wikipedia is trying to prevent this by organising professional editing and control over addition to entries.

If you're not sure whether something you read is correct, or if there is anything strange about it, check it against information on another site. Make sure you ask your tutor's opinion, too.

With large websites, it can be difficult to find what you need. Always read the whole screen – there may be several menus which are displayed in different parts of the screen.

To help you search, many large websites have:
- their own search facility or a site map that lists site content with links to the different pages
- links to similar sites where you might find more information. Clicking a link should open a new window, so you'll still be connected to the original site.

There may be useful information and links at the top, foot or either side of a web page.

There are several other useful sites you could visit when researching online.

- **Directory sites** show websites in specific categories so you can focus your search at the start.
- **Forums** are sites, or areas of a website, where people post comments on an issue. They can be useful if you want to find out opinions on a topic. You can usually read them without registering.
- **News sites** include the BBC website as well as the sites for all the daily newspapers. Check the website of your local newspaper, too.

Printing information

- Only print information that you're sure will be useful. It's easy to print too much and find yourself drowning in paper.
- Make quick notes on your print-outs so that you remember why you wanted them. It will jog your memory when you're sorting them later.
- If there's a printer-friendly option, use it. It will give you a print-out without unnecessary graphics or adverts.
- Check the bottom line of your print-outs. It should show the URL for that page of the website, and the date. You need those if you have to list your sources or if you want to quote from the page.

Researching by asking other people

You're likely to do this for two reasons:

- you need help from someone who knows a lot about a topic
- you need to find out several people's opinions on something.

TRY THIS

Go to page 90 to find out how to see how directory sites work.

TOP TIP

Bookmark sites you use regularly by adding the URL to your browser. How to do this will depend on which browser you use, eg Internet Explorer, Firefox.

Information from an expert

Explain politely why you are carrying out the investigation. Ask questions slowly and clearly about what they do and how they do it. If they don't mind, you could take written notes so you remember what they tell you. Put the name and title of the person, and the date, at the top. This is especially important if you might be seeing more than one person, to avoid getting your notes muddled up.

Ask whether you may contact them again, in case there's anything you need to check. Write down their phone number or email address. Above all, remember to say 'thank you'!

The opinions of several people

The easiest way to do this is with a questionnaire. You can either give people the questionnaire to complete themselves or interview them and complete it yourself. Professional interviewers often telephone people to ask questions, but at this stage it's not a good idea unless you know the people you're phoning and they're happy for you to do this.

TOP TIP

Design your questionnaire so that you get quantifiable answers. This means you can easily add them up to get your final result.

TRY THIS

Always test your draft questionnaire on several people, to highlight any confusing questions or instructions.

Devising a questionnaire

1. Make sure it has a title and clear instructions.

2. Rather than ask for opinions, give people options, eg yes/no, maybe/always, never/sometimes. This will make it easier to analyse the results.

3. Or you can ask interviewees to give a score, say out of 5, making it clear what each number represents, eg 5 = excellent, 4 = very good.

4. Keep your questionnaire short so that your interviewees don't lose interest. Between 10 and 15 questions is probably about right, as long as that's enough to find out all you need.

5. Remember to add 'thank you' at the end.

6. Decide upon the representative sample of people you will approach. These are the people whose views are the most relevant to the topic you're investigating.

7. Decide how many responses you need to get a valid answer. This means that the answer is representative of the wider population. For example, if you want views on food in your canteen, it's pointless only asking five people. You might pick the only five people who detest (or love) the food it serves.

Case study: Alice's research project

For an assignment, Alice needs to find information about how computer networks improve productivity both for individuals and for organisations. It is proving difficult. She has tried searching online and in her school library but has drawn a blank. She decides to ask other people for help.

Her dad knows a university professor, so she arranges to give him a call. He is very helpful and gives her a lot of information, but it is all very complex and she doesn't really understand much of what he says. She doesn't like to ask him to repeat everything, and he speaks so fast it is very hard for her to note anything down. In the end, he is not really much help at all.

After this, Alice decides to ask some of her friends and relations about how computer networks help them do things at home and at work. She creates a short questionnaire to help her collect the information she needs. Using the questionnaire, she interviews five friends and relatives who come up with lots of useful information.

- One friend says she uses the internet at home to book holidays. She finds this quicker and more convenient than going to a high street travel agent. It also makes it easier to compare prices without having to visit lots of different travel agent shops.

- Her cousin tells her that at the company where he works they sometimes have online video conferences with staff at other offices. This saves time and money as they don't need to travel to have these meetings.

- Her mum's friend explains how, at the insurance company where she works, they use email to send documents to customers. This is quicker and cheaper than posting the documents, which is what they had to do before.

Alice is very happy with the result she gets from interviewing her friends and family. They provide information that is realistic and easy to understand.

Think of ways you can use friends and family to help you find information you need for your assignments.

Keeping track of research

There is so much information available on the internet that it can be difficult to keep track of it. You should get into the habit of using your internet browser favourites to keep track of useful websites.

All web browsers allow you to create favourites (some browsers, such as Firefox, call them bookmarks). You should add all useful sites to your list of favourites whenever you come across them.

If you use different computers (eg at school, college or at home), one potential problem is that your favourites list will be different at each location and you may not have the particular favourite link available when you need it. Use the following space to make a list of your favourite sites (such as Google, Wikipedia, Microsoft Office Online, Edexcel, etc.) along with their web addresses.

Check with your friends whether they know of any other useful websites that you can add to your list. Whether you've found lots of information or only a little, assessing what you have and using it wisely is very important. This section will help you avoid the main pitfalls.

Managing your information

Whether you've found lots of information or only a little, assessing what you have and using it wisely is very important. This section will help you avoid the main pitfalls.

Organising and selecting your information

Organising your information

The first step is to organise your information so that it's easy to use.

- Make sure your written notes are neat and have a clear heading – it's often useful to date them, too.
- Note useful pages in any books or magazines you have borrowed.
- Highlight relevant parts of any handouts or leaflets.
- Work out the results of any questionnaires you've used.

Selecting your information

Re-read the **assignment brief** or instructions you were given to remind yourself of the exact wording of the question(s) and divide your information into three groups:

1 Information that is totally relevant.

2 Information that is not as good, but could come in useful.

3 Information that doesn't match the questions or assignment brief very much but that you kept because you couldn't find anything better!

Check there are no obvious gaps in your information against the questions or assignment brief. If there are, make a note of them so that you know exactly what you still have to find. Although it's ideal to have everything you need before you start work, don't delay if you're short of time.

Putting your information in order

Putting your information in a logical order means you can find what you want easily. It will save you time in the long run. This is doubly important if you have lots of information and will be doing the work over several sessions.

As a learner on an IT course, you will have a lot of information stored in computer files. This will include lesson notes, assignment briefs and assignment work, information downloaded from the internet, homework and class tasks, etc. You may also have different versions of the assignment you are currently working on. Keeping track of all this information can be difficult, even more so if you work on several different computers and have some files stored on each computer and perhaps also on a USB memory stick. It is important that you organise your files and stored information so that you can find items easily when required to do so.

Activity: Organising your files

There are a number of ways in which you can organise your files efficiently:

1. Try to store files in one place. Storing your files in lots of different locations is confusing as you will need to remember where you have stored the latest version. Probably the best approach is to store all your work on a USB memory stick so you can use your files on any computer. Always remember to back up your files.

2. Create and use a logical folder structure, perhaps based on the different units you will be studying.

3. Use a method for naming files that makes it easy to know what is in each one. Try to use meaningful names, such as

   Unit 2 Assignment 1 Task 2

   Remember, file names can be up to 255 characters long.

   Calling your files Doc1 or Work or School doesn't give much clue as to what the files contains.

4. Practise using the search facilities that Windows provides.

When you view a folder, you can display the documents in date order with the most recently modified displaying first.

Click on the View menu and choose 'details'

Then click on 'Date Modified' to display the most recently saved documents. Click it again to show the oldest documents

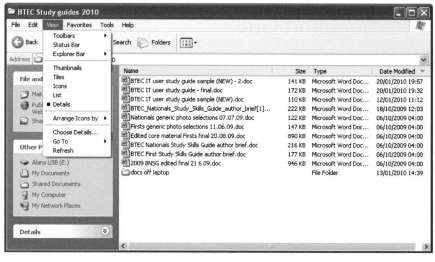

You can also search for individual documents.

Click the 'Search' icon

Then click 'Documents'

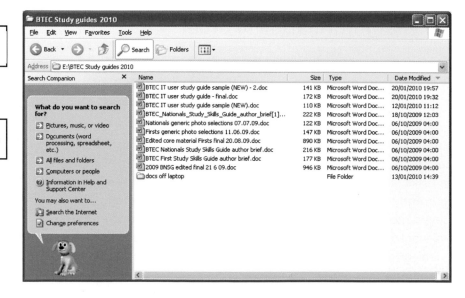

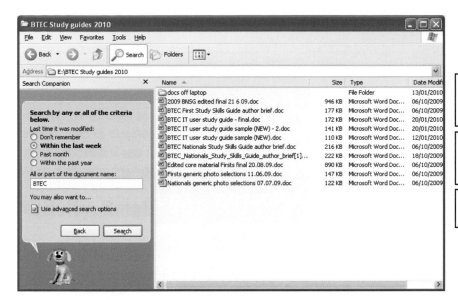

Then choose the last time you think the document was saved…

If you click 'Use advanced search options' you will see the options shown below

…and all or part of the document name

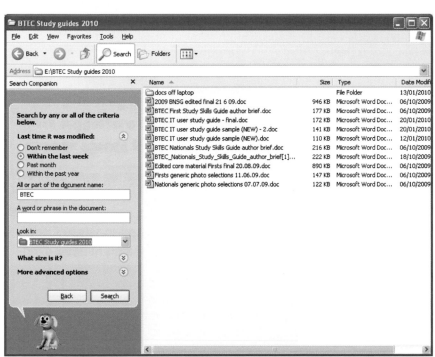

'Advanced search options' allows you to search for a word or phrase that is in the document and to search only in a particular folder or disk. Remember, searching the whole of the C: drive or My Documents will take several minutes if you have a lot of files

Finally, click the 'Search' button and wait while the search is done

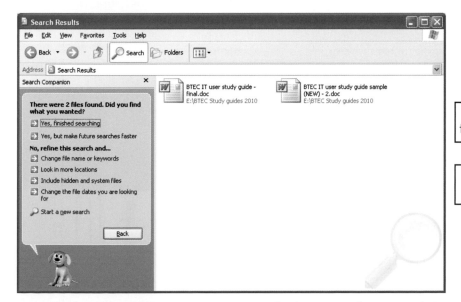

These are the search results. The two files above matched the criteria entered

You can use these options to modify your search and try again

Microsoft product screenshots on pages 50–1 reprinted with permission from Microsoft Corporation.

Using a desktop search program

If you have got a lot of files and find it difficult to locate them on your computer or memory stick, you can use a desktop search program to find what you are looking for. There are a number of desktop search programs, many of which are available for free download. Google, for example, provides Google Desktop as a free trial download. Desktop search programs are usually much faster at finding files than a standard Windows search.

Case study: Winston's course file

Surrounded by newspapers, magazines and the internet we sometimes suffer from what is called 'information overload' – we are exposed to too much information and become unsure about what is really appropriate or relevant to us. How can you filter out irrelevant information and focus on items that are really useful and important?

Winston wants to keep up to date with IT and find information to help him with his assignments. He visits the library regularly to read newspapers and magazines, and he also checks websites like the BBC news technology site. However, he is finding it difficult to keep track of all the information.

'The problem is that, when I have an assignment that needs a certain piece of information, I know I've read something that is relevant, but I can't always remember where or when. So I've decided to keep a folder, which I've divided into the different units I'm doing. Now

when I find an article I think may be relevant, or just interesting, I copy it or print it and put it in my folder. I also keep a general section in my folder for information that I think is important or relevant but I'm not sure what unit it might relate to.'

Winston's folder is a very useful resource. Not only does it help him with his assignments, it also helps him keep up to date with the important issues in IT. The folder will also help him if he progresses to study a BTEC National in IT or if he decides to go to university. This method of collecting important and interesting information will also prove useful when it comes to applying for jobs because employers want people who are interested in IT and are well informed about the important issues in the industry.

What information would be useful to you on your course? How could you organise this information to make accessing it easier?

Organising other information and paperwork

Although much of the information you collect and work with will be in the form of computer files, you also need to keep quite a lot of paper information. This includes such general information as your timetable, unit-specific information such as notes and handouts your tutor gives you, assignment briefs and any partially completed work you have printed.

It is really important to keep this paperwork well organised. You should use a ring binder folder to do this. Use a set of card dividers to split the folder into sections for each unit so that you can insert papers where they belong. Make sure you write the unit number/name on the divider tab.

Don't let paperwork pile up in the bottom of your bag where it will get messy and you will forget which unit it belongs to. Keep your folder and hole-punch with you at all times. Write your name and mobile phone number clearly on the front of the folder so that if you should leave it somewhere it will hopefully be returned to you. Losing your folder would be a disaster!

Use this checklist to make sure you have all the tools you need to organise your work.

Organisational checklist
☐ I have a suitable ring binder folder.
☐ My name and mobile phone number is clearly on my folder.
☐ I have dividers to split my folder up by units.
☐ I have labelled all the dividers by unit.
☐ I have a hole-punch.
☐ I have put all my paperwork in the correct section.

Remember, information is knowledge! It really is. Treat the paper-based information you receive from your tutor with respect – keep it safe and well organised so you can get the maximum benefit from it.

> **TOP TIP**
>
> Buy a hole-punch. This allows you to punch holes in paperwork so that you can file it in the right place in your folder straight away.

Interpreting and presenting your information

The next stage is to use your information to prepare the document and/or oral presentation you have to give. There are four steps:

1 Understand what you're reading.
2 Interpret what you're reading.
3 Know the best form in which to produce the information, bearing in mind the purpose for which it is required.
4 Create the required document so that it's in a suitable layout with correct spelling and punctuation.

Understanding what you read

As a general rule, never use information that you don't understand. However, nobody understands complex or unfamiliar material the first time they read it, especially if they just scan through it quickly. Before you reject it, try this:

Read it once to get the main idea.	Read it again, slowly, to try to take in more detail.	Look up any words you don't know in a dictionary to find out what they mean.
Write your own version.	Summarise the main points in your own words.	Read it a third time and underline or highlight the main points. (If this is a book or magazine that you shouldn't write in, take a photocopy first and write on that.)

Special note: Show both the article and your own version to your tutor to check your understanding. This will help you identify any points you missed out and help you improve your skills of interpreting and summarising.

Understanding unfamiliar information

BTEC FACT

In your assignments, it's better to separate opinions from facts. If you're quoting someone's views, make this clear. (See also page 56.)

Interpreting what you read

Interpreting what you read is different from understanding it. This is because you can't always take it for granted that something you read means what it says. The writer may have had a very strong or biased opinion, or may have exaggerated for effect. This doesn't mean that you can't use the information, but you will need to add an explanation.

Strong opinions and bias

People often have strong points of view about certain topics. This may be based on reliable facts, but not always! We can all jump to conclusions that may not be very logical, especially if we feel strongly about something.

Things aren't always what they seem to be. Are these boys fighting or are they having a good time?

Exaggeration

Many newspapers exaggerate facts to startle and attract their readers.

LOCAL FIRM DOUBLES STAFF IN TWO WEEKS!

This newspaper headline sounds very positive. You could easily think it means employment is growing and there are more jobs in your area. Then you read on, and find the firm had only four staff and now has eight!

Tables and graphs

You need to be able to interpret what the figures mean, especially when you look at differences between columns or rows. For example, your friend might have an impressive spreadsheet that lists his income and expenditure. In reality, it doesn't tell you much until you add the figures up and subtract one from the other. Only then can you say whether he is getting into debt. And even if he is, you need to see his budget over a few months, rather than just one which may be exceptional.

Choosing a format

You may have been given specific instructions about the format and layout of a document you have to produce, in which case life is easy as long as you follow them! If not, think carefully about the best way to set out your information so that it is clear.

TRY THIS

There are many scare stories in the media about issues such as immigration, children's reading ability or obesity. Next time you're watching television and these are discussed, see if you can spot biased views, exaggeration and claims without any supporting evidence.

TOP TIP

Never make assumptions or jump to conclusions. Make sure you have all the evidence to support your views.

Different formats	Example
text	when you write in paragraphs or prepare a report or summary
graphical	a diagram, graph or chart
pictorial	a drawing, photograph, cartoon or pictogram
tabular	numerical information in a table

The best method(s) will depend on the information you have, the source(s) of your material and the purpose of the document – a leaflet for schoolchildren needs graphics and pictures to make it lively, whereas a report to company shareholders would be mainly in text form with just one or two graphs.

Stating your sources

Whatever format you use, if you are including other people's views, comments or opinions, or copying a table or diagram from another publication, you must state the source by including the name of the author, publication or the web address. This can be in the text or as part of a list at the end. Failure to do this (so you are really pretending other people's work is your own) is known as **plagiarism**. Plagiarism is a serious offence with penalties to match.

Text format

Creating written documents gets easier with practice. These points should help.

TOP TIP

Don't just rely on your spellchecker. It won't find a word spelled wrongly that makes another valid word (eg from/form), so you must proofread everything. You should also check whether your spellchecker is set to check American English or British English. There are some spelling differences.

Golden rules for written documents

1 Think about who will be reading it, then write in an appropriate language and style.

2 Ensure it is technically correct, ie no wrong spellings or bad punctuation.

3 Take time to make it look good, with clear headings, consistent spacing and plenty of white space.

4 Write in paragraphs, each with a different theme. Leave a line space between each one.

5 If you have a lot of separate points to mention, use bullets or numbered points. Numbered points show a certain order or quantity (step 1, step 2, etc). Use bullet points when there is no suggested order.

6 Only use words that you understand the meaning of, or it might look as if you don't know what you mean.

7 Structure your document so that it has a beginning, middle and end.

8 Prepare a draft and ask your tutor to confirm you are on the right track and are using your information in the best way.

Activity: Structure a document

This activity is designed to show you how to structure a report; with an introduction, middle and summary. Write a short piece about how you coped with your first assignment using the table headings and questions for guidance.

Introduction How did you feel when you started the assignment? What were your expectations of the task?	
Middle What progress did you make on the task? How did your approach develop during the course of the assignment? How hard was it?	
Summary How much did you achieve? What grades did you get? What would you do differently to improve your performance in future assignments?	

Try this activity again after you have completed several more assignments.
Are you making progress in your approach to assignments?

TRY THIS

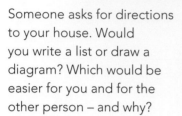

Someone asks for directions to your house. Would you write a list or draw a diagram? Which would be easier for you and for the other person – and why?

Graphical format

Most people find graphics better than a long description for creating a quick picture in the viewer's mind. There are several types of graphical format, and you can easily produce any of these if you have good ICT skills.

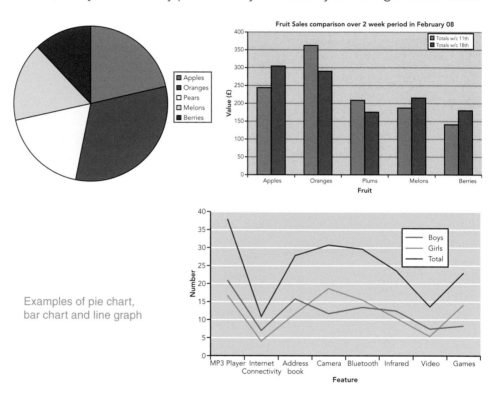

Examples of pie chart, bar chart and line graph

Pictorial format

Newspapers and magazines use pictures to illustrate situations and reduce the amount of words needed. It doesn't always have to be photographs though. For example, a new building may be sketched to show what it will look like.

A pictogram or pictograph is another type of pictorial format, such as charts which use the image of an object (fruit, coins, even pizzas) to represent data, such as the number eaten or amount spent.

TOP TIP

Don't spend hours writing text when an illustration can do the job better. However, you must make sure that the illustration you choose is suitable for the document and for the reader.

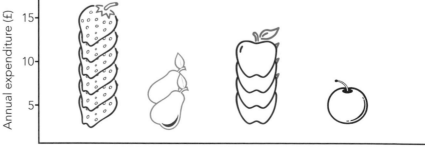

Tabular format

A table can be an easy way to communicate information. Imagine a retailer preparing information about the items in stock. Text would be difficult to understand and comparisons between stock levels and sales would be almost impossible to make. A table, however, would easily show the fastest-selling items.

Tables are also ideal if you are showing rankings – such as best-selling music or books.

Bestsellers list – September 2009

Position	Title	Author	Imprint	Publication
1 (New)	Lost Symbol, The	Brown, Dan	Bantam Press	15-Sep-2009
2 (1)	Complaints, The	Rankin, Ian	Orion	03-Sep-2009
3 (New)	Return Journey, The	Binchy, Maeve	Orion	17-Sep-2009
4 (7)	Sapphire	Price, Katie	Century	30-Jul-2009
5 (9)	Wolf Hall	Mantel, Hilary	Fourth Estate	30-Apr-2009
6 (3)	Week in December, A	Faulks, Sebastian	Hutchinson	03-Sep-2009
7 (2)	Alex Cross's Trial	Patterson, James	Century	10-Sep-2009
8 (4)	White Queen, The	Gregory, Philippa	Simon & Schuster Ltd	18-Aug-2009
9 (5)	Even Money	Francis, Dick & Francis, Felix	Michael Joseph	03-Sep-2009
10 (8)	206 Bones	Reichs, Kathy	William Heinemann	27-Aug-2009

National newspaper circulation – September 2009

	August 2009	August 2008	% change on last year	August 09 (without bulks)	March 2009 – August 2009	% change on last year
Sun	3,128,501	3,148,792	-0.64	3,128,501	3,052,480	-2.25
Daily Mail	2,171,686	2,258,843	-3.86	2,044,079	2,178,462	-4.45
Daily Mirror	1,324,883	1,455,270	-8.96	1,324,883	1,331,108	9.44
Daily Star	886,814	751,494	18.01	886,814	855,511	16.65
The Daily Telegraph	814,087	860,298	-5.37	722,644	807,328	-6.73
Daily Express	730,234	748,664	-2.46	730,234	727,824	-1.32
Times	576,185	612,779	-5.97	529,746	588,471	-4.63
Financial Times	395,845	417,570	-5.2	365,269	411,098	-6.7
Daily Record	347,302	390,197	-10.99	345,277	350,306	-10.59
Guardian	311,387	332,587	-6.37	311,387	332,790	-4.11
Independent	187,837	230,033	-18.34	148,551	198,445	-16.76

Activity: Interpreting and presenting information

IT provides many different ways to interpret and present information, for example:

- **Spreadsheets**
  to present numbers and include totals, averages, etc
  to present numbers using graphs and charts
- **Presentation programs (eg PowerPoint)**
  to create slides of text, figures, diagrams and graphs for presentation to an audience
- **Word processing programs**
  to create reports that combine text and graphics
  to create tables of text and figures
- **Desktop publishing programs**
  to create documents such as posters and leaflets.

With all these different options, which IT tool is best suited to a particular situation? Match the tools listed above to the tasks listed below. (In some cases, more than one IT tool may be appropriate.)

Task	IT tool
Creating a timetable to show which lessons you have on each day of the week	
Comparing the costs of different internet service providers	
Showing your classmates the results of your research	
Producing a poster about health and safety issues when using computers	
Analysing the results of a questionnaire	

Activity: Choosing a laptop

Your friend is not studying IT at college and she doesn't know much about computers. However, she needs to use IT for her course and has asked you to recommend a suitable laptop for her to use at college and at home.

1   What key features would you recommend that your friend needs in her laptop?

2   Research at least *three* possible different laptops you could recommend and list them below. Identify the specifications for the key features you selected above.

3   For each of the key features, use a **different** method to present the information you have found; for example, a bar chart, a pie diagram or table.

4   Ask a number of your classmates to look at the different ways in which you have presented the information and to give you feedback on which method allowed them to compare the different laptops most easily.

You can use this information to guide your choice of method when you need to present numerical data in the future.

Making presentations

Presentations help you to learn communication skills.

Some people hate the idea of standing up to speak in front of an audience. This is quite normal, and you can use the extra energy from nerves to improve your performance.

Presentations aren't some form of torture devised by your tutor! They are included in your course because they help you learn many skills, such as speaking in public and preparing visual aids. They also help you practise working as a team member and give you a practical reason for researching information. And it can be far more enjoyable to talk about what you've found out rather than write about it!

There's a knack to preparing and giving a presentation so that you use your energies well, don't waste time, don't fall out with everyone around you and keep your stress levels as low as possible. Think about the task in three stages: preparation, organisation and delivery.

Preparation

Start your initial preparations as soon as you can. Putting them off will only cause problems later. Discuss the task in your team so that everyone is clear about what has to be done and how long you have to do it in.

Divide any research fairly among the team, allowing for people's strengths and weaknesses. You'll also need to agree:

- which visual aids would be best
- which handouts you need and who should prepare them
- where and when the presentation will be held, and what you should wear
- what questions you might be asked, both individually and as a team, and how you should prepare for them.

Once you've decided all this, carry out the tasks you've been allocated to the best of your ability and by the deadline agreed.

TOP TIP

Keep visual aids simple but effective and check any handouts carefully before you make lots of copies.

Organisation

This is about the planning you need to do as a team so that everything will run smoothly on the day.

Delivery

This refers to your performance during the presentation. Being well prepared and well organised helps stop you panicking. If you're very nervous at the start, take a few deep breaths and concentrate on the task, not yourself. It's quite normal to be nervous at the start but this usually fades once you get under way. You might even enjoy it …

Ahmed and Simon's presentation experiences

Ahmed is worried. He has to give a presentation to the rest of the class. It is the first time this skill has come up and he is finding it a daunting prospect. Simon, on the other hand, is confident. He has lots of information and it is a subject he knows well.

The presentation is part of an assignment and all the learners have to create PowerPoint slides to accompany their presentations. Each speaker is allowed just 10 minutes for their presentation but Simon wants to squeeze as much information in as he can – after all, that's what a presentation is for, to show what you know, isn't it?

Ahmed speaks to his tutor to get some ideas about how to do a presentation and he gets some good advice:

- Your presentation should have a structure with a beginning (introduction), middle (the main content) and an end (summary).
- When you create the slides for your presentation, you should only include the key headings rather than all the information.

- You should make short notes to remind yourself what you are going to say. Use these notes as a prompt rather than reading off your slides.
- Rehearse what you are going to say before you give your presentation. This will also help you keep to the time allowed.

On the day of the presentation, Simon's doesn't go too well. He has created 30 slides, all packed with information which is too small for the audience to read. The tutor stops Simon's presentation after 12 slides, otherwise it will be much longer than the 10 minutes allowed. Ahmed's presentation goes more smoothly. He is nervous but his notes help as doesn't have to read from the slides. His slides are clear and easy to read – with just the main points on them. He has a good introduction to the presentation and doesn't run out of time.

How good are your PowerPoint skills? How can you make sure that you know enough of the features of PowerPoint to give a good, engaging presentation?

TOP TIP

Never read from prepared prompt cards! Look at the audience when you're talking and smile occasionally. If you need to use prompt cards as a reminder, make sure they are clear so that you need only glance at them.

TOP TIP

Remember, the audience always makes allowances for some nerves!

TOP TIP

When making a PowerPoint presentation, don't just read out what it says on the slides. The audience can read! Use the slides as prompt cards.

Activity: Presenting an IT area of interest

This activity allows you to plan a presentation on an area of IT that interests you (for example, computer games, graphics and media or the internet). You should include information about your qualifications, personality and experience to help explain why this area interests you.

Use the table below to plan what information you will include in your introduction, the main part of the presentation and the summary.

Section	Information to include
Introduction	
Main presentation	
Summary	

Now use the space below to sketch out the information you will include on each slide. Remember, the slides should include only the main headings, not the detailed information you will talk about in your presentation. Aim for one introductory slide, about four or five main slides, and one summary slide.

Introduction	Main slide 1
Main slide 2	Main slide 3
Main slide 4	Main slide 5
Summary slide	

Now use presentation software, such as PowerPoint, to create your slides. You should write separate notes that list what you will say in detail.

Practise your presentation in front of your friends or family and ask them for suggestions on how to improve it.

Your assessments

The importance of assignments

All learners on BTEC First courses are assessed by means of **assignments**. Each one is designed to link to specific **learning outcomes** and **grading criteria**. At the end of the course, your assignment grades put together determine your overall grade.

To get the best grade you can, you need to know the golden rules that apply to all assignments, then how to interpret the specific instructions.

10 golden rules for assignments

1. Check that you understand the instructions.

2. Check whether you have to do all the work on your own, or if you will do some as a member of a group. If you work as a team, you need to identify which parts are your own contributions.

3. Always write down any verbal instructions you are given.

4. Check the final deadline and any penalties for not meeting it.

5. Make sure you know what to do if you have a serious personal problem, eg illness, and need an official extension.

6. Copying someone else's work (**plagiarism**) is a serious offence and is easy for experienced tutors to spot. It's never worth the risk.

7. Schedule enough time for finding out the information and doing initial planning.

8. Allow plenty of time between talking to your tutor about your plans, preparations and drafts and the final deadline.

9. Don't panic if the assignment seems long or complicated. Break it down into small, manageable chunks.

10. If you suddenly get stuck, ask your tutor to talk things through with you.

Case study: Understanding command words

Silvia is starting her first assignment for Unit 2: Working in the IT Industry, and she really wants to do well. The task covering P1 is pretty straightforward: it requires her to describe common employee attributes. Looking at the unit specification, she can see what sort of attributes she has to cover, and she provides a paragraph describing each attribute and also gives an example.

The merit criteria are a bit more involved. To achieve M2, for example, Silvia needs to explain how certain attributes are important for specific job roles. She tells her friend: 'To be honest, to start with I didn't really think there was much difference between describing and explaining something. Then I spoke to my tutor and he told me that explaining involves saying **why** something is the case. So for this merit criterion I need to say why a particular employee attribute is important for a certain job.'

Describe and **explain** are examples of command words that are found at the start of each grading criterion. Understanding the difference between them is important to meeting the grade.

The following is a small section of Slivia's first attempt at the merit criterion.

'For a job like an IT hardware repair technician, attributes such as good investigation and troubleshooting skills would be important.'

When she speaks to her tutor and shows him what she has done so far he points out that this is really a description and doesn't explain why these skills would be important.

This is her improved version:

'For a job like an IT hardware repair technician, attributes such as good investigation and troubleshooting skills would be important. This is because when trying to repair a faulty computer they would need to investigate what the problem is and use their troubleshooting skills to identify what was causing the fault.'

By adding explanations to each of her examples of attributes relating to a specific job, Silvia was able to meet the M2 criterion.

Look at some of the other grading criteria for Unit 2. Can you see the difference between what is required for the pass, merit and distinction criteria?

Interpreting the instructions

Most assignments start with a **command word** – describe, explain, evaluate, etc. These words relate to how complex the answer should be.

Command words

Learners often don't do their best because they read the command words but don't understand exactly what they have to do. The tables on the following pages show you what is required for each grade when you see a particular command word.

Command words and obtaining a pass

Complete ...	Complete a form, diagram or drawing.
Demonstrate ...	Show that you can do a particular activity.
Describe ...	Give a clear, straightforward description that includes all the main points.
Identify ...	Give all the basic facts relating to a certain topic.
List ...	Write a list of the main items (not sentences).
Name ...	State the proper terms related to a drawing or diagram.
Outline ...	Give all the main points, but without going into too much detail.
State ...	Point out or list the main features.

Examples:

- **List** the main features on your mobile phone.
- **Describe** the best way to greet a customer.
- **Outline** the procedures you follow to keep your computer system secure.

Command words and obtaining a merit

Analyse ...	Identify the factors that apply, and state how these are linked and how each of them relates to the topic.
Comment on ...	Give your own opinions or views.
Compare ... Contrast ...	Identify the main factors relating to two or more items and point out the similarities and differences.
Competently use ...	Take full account of information and feedback you have obtained to review or improve an activity.
Demonstrate ...	Prove you can carry out a more complex activity.
Describe ...	Give a full description including details of all the relevant features.
Explain ...	Give logical reasons to support your views.
Justify ...	Give reasons for the points you are making so that the reader knows what you're thinking.
Suggest ...	Give your own ideas or thoughts.

Examples:

- **Explain** why mobile phones are so popular.
- **Describe** the needs of four different types of customers.
- **Suggest** the type of procedures your employer would need to introduce to keep the IT system secure.

TRY THIS

Check the command word you are likely to see for each of your units in the **grading grid** in advance. This tells you the **grading criteria** for the unit so that you know the evidence you will have to present.

Command words and obtaining a distinction

Analyse ...	Identify several relevant factors, show how they are linked, and explain the importance of each.
Compare ... Contrast ...	Identify the main factors in two or more situations, then explain the similarities and differences, and in some cases say which is best and why.
Demonstrate ...	Prove that you can carry out a complex activity taking into account information you have obtained or received to adapt your original idea.
Describe ...	Give a comprehensive description which tells a story to the reader and shows that you can apply your knowledge and information correctly.
Evaluate ...	Bring together all your information and make a judgement on the importance or success of something.
Explain ...	Provide full details and reasons to support the arguments you are making.
Justify ...	Give full reasons or evidence to support your opinion.
Recommend ...	Weigh up all the evidence to come to a conclusion, with reasons, about what would be best.

Examples:

- **Evaluate** the features and performance of your mobile phone.
- **Analyse** the role of customer service in contributing to an organisation's success.
- **Justify** the main features on the website of a large, successful organisation of your choice.

TOP TIP

Think of assignments as an opportunity to demonstrate what you've learned and to get useful feedback about your work.

Activity: Pass, merit or distinction?

By now, you should have a folder for your course with dividers for each unit. Find the course specification on the Edexcel website and print the page for each unit showing the grading criteria grid. Put this in the appropriate section of your folder.

You should have a list of the assignments you will need to complete to cover each unit, and when they are due to be completed. Use the table below to record this information. You can ask your tutor for help if there is anything you are unsure about.

Unit title		
	Due date	Grading criteria covered
Assignment 1		
Assignment 2		
Assignment 3		
Unit title		
	Due date	Grading criteria covered
Assignment 1		
Assignment 2		
Assignment 3		
Unit title		
	Due date	Grading criteria covered
Assignment 1		
Assignment 2		
Assignment 3		
Unit title		
	Due date	Grading criteria covered
Assignment 1		
Assignment 2		
Assignment 3		

Unit title		
	Due date	Grading criteria covered
Assignment 1		
Assignment 2		
Assignment 3		
Unit title		
	Due date	Grading criteria covered
Assignment 1		
Assignment 2		
Assignment 3		

Sample assignment

Front sheet

Make sure you complete the front sheet properly, entering your name clearly and signing and dating it at the bottom.

It's important to submit your assignment before the deadline. Check you centre's policy on meeting deadlines.

It's a good idea to ask your tutor to check your work before submitting it, as you may have forgotten something important.

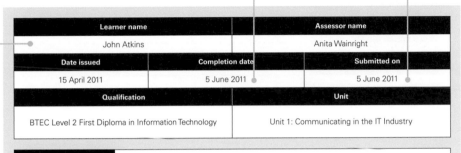

Learner name			Assessor name	
John Atkins			Anita Wainright	

Date issued	Completion date		Submitted on	
15 April 2011	5 June 2011		5 June 2011	

Qualification		Unit		
BTEC Level 2 First Diploma in Information Technology		Unit 1: Communicating in the IT Industry		

Assignment title | Specialist Communication Channels

In this assessment you will have opportunities to provide evidence against the following criteria. Indicate the page numbers where the evidence can be found.

Criteria reference	To achieve the criteria the evidence must show that the learner is able to:	Task no.	Evidence
P5	Select, set up and use a specialist communication channel to communicate and exchange information	2	Page 2
P6	Explain the social impacts of the use of IT	1	Page 1
M1	Justify why a specialist communication channel is effective for a given purpose	2	Page 2
M2	Discuss the potential threats which the use of IT has introduced	1	Page 1
D1	Explain how to ensure safe and secure use of a specialist communication channel	2	Page 3

Learner declaration

I certify that the work submitted for this assignment is my own and research sources are fully acknowledged.

Learner signature: *John Atkins*   Date: *5 June 2011*

You must check that the evidence you submit meets the requirements of each of these grading criteria.

The evidence you provide must be your own work, not copied from anywhere else. Where you do quote books, articles, etc. you must include a reference to the original source.

You must provide specific evidence to cover each of the grading criteria in this assignment, you need to list the pages in your assignment where the evidence is located.

Assignment brief

Remember that the assignment is about communicating effectively using IT, and the social impacts of IT.

The scenario helps you relate your assignment work to the sort of task you might do in a real IT job.

Unit title	Unit 1: Communicating in the IT Industry
Qualification	Edexcel BTEC Level 2 First Diploma in Information Technology
Start date	15 April 2011
Deadline date	5 June 2011
Assessor	Anita Wainright

Assignment title	Specialist Communication Channels

The purpose of this assignment is to:
Allow learners the opportunity to develop their communication skills and knowledge in the IT sector for either progression onto a higher course or to prepare them for employment positions in IT-related work placements. Learners will develop their use of IT and demonstrate how technology can aid effective communication while also looking into the different ways IT has had an impact on individuals, communities and society.

Scenario
As the world keeps turning and the people and the life they lead around it change, so does the knowledge and the development of technology and the way we speak to one another. Every day we are surrounded by advertisements bending our way of thinking to make us want more and more products and services. We upgrade our phones to the latest model available as soon as our monthly contracts are due for renewal. We use that new car insurance comparison website that was advertised on TV, because we saw the commercial and now can't get the tune out of our heads.

How do advertisers do it? How do the sales and marketing teams in large organisations know just how to get the right audience to purchase the right product? How does our employer know just how to get the team to do the jobs he/she needs them to do, and on time?

The key is communication and the way we use the tools at our disposal to get the greatest level of productivity out of our employees. A positive approach is needed in the workplace, and in a rapidly changing environment such as an IT office, web design studio or games design company, it is essential to communicate in the language that the employees understand. In this situation, you have to use IT tools effectively. Use them incorrectly and you will lose your audience in moments; use them correctly and the IT industry is your career ladder ready and waiting for you to climb it.

For this assignment, imagine you are working in a web design office, called 'Inspiration', based in the North West. Every week new and varied clients come along wanting new websites designed from scratch. The clients have chosen Inspiration because it is based in the North and can tailor website designs to suit the northern consumer market. For example, Inspiration has previously designed sites for a new florist that opened in the Manchester area, it has provided an upgrade to the website of the outdoor activity shop Walkabout in Ambleside, and it has provided graphics and improved a website that was already in place for a young student, based in Liverpool, who wanted to teach a musical instrument as a part-time job when not in college.

Task 1
To achieve P6 – explain the social impacts of the use of IT
To achieve M2 – discuss the potential threats which the use of IT has introduced
As with any form of communication, it is crucial that people can understand and interpret what you are trying to say and that there are no negative connotations in any documents that you produce. Inspiration is a family-friendly company and likes all its employees to feel valued and appreciated. It prides itself on the accuracy and fluency in which its newsletter keeps its employees updated every month with activities, social events, achievements, current company advances and the impact that these will have on its employees.

You have been asked to provide a written article for the 'current company advances' section in the next edition of the newsletter. In the article you will be expected to talk about how the company's developments in IT have had an impact on the social network of its employees and consumers, explaining their effects on local communities, economic development and employment structure. You should also include new threats to the company that people need to be aware of due to the increasing use of IT, such as cyber bullying, spam and phishing.

This task is about the ways IT has an impact on people and the potential dangers of using IT.

This task is about setting up and using an online forum or other method of electronic communication.

To justify the effectiveness of the communication method you set up and use, you can consider why it is better than other more traditional methods of communication.

Use whatever tools or resources that you have at your disposal to produce the article, and remember to include pictures to make the article attractive to the audience that will be reading it.

What will you need to submit as evidence:
For P6 and M2 – the final version of the article.

Task 2
To achieve P5 – select, set up and use a specialist communication channel to communicate and exchange information
In order to prove to the manager you are worthy of a promotion you are to develop something for the company that will increase the communication within the team. He has suggested you try to encourage the team to use and contribute to an online forum, wiki or another form of electronic communication. The employees must be able to access it at any time and they must feel comfortable using it to discuss matters of the workplace. It must be secure as company information should not be published and should not become public knowledge. (Examples include Ning, Google Docs, wikis and video conferencing.) You will need to provide evidence that you chose, set up and used the forum, wiki or another form of electronic communication yourself by documenting each step of the process. This could be done using screenshots.

To achieve M1 – justify why a specialist communication channel is effective for a given purpose
Explain why you chose your particular specialist communication channel in a brief report to the manager. You will need to justify any points that you make and ensure that you have clearly shown why you chose that method over any other. Talk about the pros and cons of the suggested communication method in relation to Inspiration.

To achieve D1 – explain how to ensure safe and secure use of a specialist communication channel
And finally your manager needs to know that this method of communication is safe and secure. By adding to the report, explain to him how the specialist communication channel is safe and secure and how it will benefit the company. Remember to highlight any issues that may occur and suggest contingency plans in case security and information is hacked into.

What will you need to submit as evidence:
For P5 – show how you chose and set up the communication channel – for this you could use screenshots. Also show screenshots or printouts of a discussion that you have participated in using this channel of communication.

For M1 and D1 – a report discussing the specialist communication channel you chose for P5 and how safe this method of communicating is for the company to use.

Sources of information

Textbooks
Shmerling, Leah – *Communication in the Workplace* (Macmillan Education Australia Pty Ltd, 1996) ISBN: 0-7329-1941-XD
Darling, Ann L, Dannels, Deanna P – *Practicing Engineers Talk about the Importance of Talk: A Report on the Role of Oral Communication in the Workplace*, Volume 52, Issue 1, (Communication Education, 2003)

This brief has been verified as being fit for purpose.			
Assessor	Anita Wainright		
Signature	*Anita Wainright*	Date	*13 April 2011*
Internal verifier	Ron Woodward		
Signature	*Ron Woodward*	Date	*13 April 2011*

Check the unit content to make sure you have covered all the required aspects of safety and security.

You should also be able to find lots of information about the safety and security issues related to your choice of specialist communication channel on the Internet.

Sample learner work

These newsletter articles cover P6 and M2.

Sample learner work: page 1

Task 1

Inspiration   Volume 1, Issue 12   Page 8

Our social network and our customers

Inspiration prides itself on being a family based organisation that does whatever it can to ensure happy, healthy working employees. Our mission statement is '…to be an inspiration to our family. Our family is our employees, our customers and our environment. If we take care of these, they will take care of us.' One of the greatest gifts we can share with our employees is to improve our technology to make life easier.

Inspiration has made many developments recently in its use of IT at work and this has had an impact on the social network of our employees and our consumers. Customers are making use of our online website and the free trial download, 'sample your own website'. It is allowing customers to design basic layouts and view sample websites before they book a consultation with one of our representatives. Local communities are going to be able to design and style their websites just how they want and be able to compare to similar local businesses and rival competitors.

Some of our employees are finding that they can now use the company laptops to work from home, keeping in constant contact with their bosses and their families throughout the day. The investment in these machines, are meaning that productivity in the company is greater and staff are mentally feeling happier in their jobs. And as you would expect this kind of good work is going to be re-warded for those who work on performance related pay when the Christmas bonuses come along.

With happy customers and happy employees, the company is constantly monitoring its economic development, improving discipline procedures, improving employment structure and generally focussing on the overall development and expansion of the company. We are especially watching the access to the company network and the restrictions policy is being amended. Although we can trust our employees, it's the outside hackers that we can't and if the company is to expand nationally, or globally in the next few years, we need to be prepared.

Author: J, Atkins

"Looking after our well-being…."

IT security threats – some solutions to make you feel safe:

1) Delete suspicious emails without opening them.

2) When using social networking sites, ignore friend requests and block them if you don't know who they are.

3) Never give personal information in a reply to an email or over the internet.

4) Block spam messages using your browser or download spam blocking software off the internet, eg AVG internet security.

5) Remember, think safe and be safe.

Cyber Bullying, Spam and Phishing: Are we prepared?

If anybody using the work computers, or doing work at home on the new laptops has not heard of the following (cyber bullying, spam and phishing) and are protecting themselves from them, then this part of the article is very important to you.

Cyber bullying: Is basically bullying through the use of online websites. So the most popular way would be through social networking sites like, Facebook, Beebo and MSN. This way of bullying could take place in work or at home in your social life and at any age.

Spam: Is when messages are sent over the internet many times over to people who don't really want it. A good example of this is companies advertising and sending to any active email address the find and also chain emails that require you to forward on the message.

Phishing: Is when people manage to virtually pretend to be someone else, get information about your accounts, credit cards or even your address, and then use to illegally to access whatever they wish, usually usually your money. To see an example, visit http://www.privacyrights.org/ar/phishing.htm#example This is an example of an eBay phishing email.

The Google Docs page and the screen shots provide evidence for P5.

Sample learner work: page 2

Task 2

- **P5 evidence** – select, set up and use a specialist communication channel to communicate and exchange information

Using Google Docs will increase the communication within the team. I have asked the team to use and contribute to an online spreadsheet that I made to look like a forum. I chose a spreadsheet because I know we all know how to use it already. It was accessible at any time. Google Docs is as secure as the user makes it so I made everyone read the, 'Google – Keeping your data secure' webpage before they were allowed to contribute to the forum I set up. This page can be found at: www.google.com/help/security/index.html#utm__campaign=en&utm__source=en-ha-ww-ww-bk-cn&utm__medium=ha&utm__term=google%20security.

[The learner supplied screenshots of Google Documents, with accompanying call-out captions, explaining how he created his own Google Documents account, how he uploaded a spreadsheet file to Google Documents, and how he had a discussion about the spreadsheet through Google Documents.]

Task 2

- **M1 evidence** – justify why a specialist communication channel is effective for a given purpose
- **D1 evidence** – explain how to ensure safe and secure use of a specialist communication channel

Why I chose this specialist communication channel (M1):

I think this a really good way to communicate for people who know about using IT software. The Inspiration company are going to always be on the internet during the day because they make websites for a living. They have 24/7 access to Google and it is a recognised search engine. By using this, the staff members can access any document and make alterations to it, save it and there is only ever the one master copy so everybody knows where they are up to. It can also be used for other tasks, say the team are struggling with a piece of code that they writing for one of the websites, they can put it on Google docs for the whole team to look at and they can share ideas on how to solve the problem.

It's a way of bringing the team closer together and allowing them to work together wherever they are. It would be better for this team to use Google docs because it is more accessible than say a intranet forum and whereas Google docs takes seconds to set up, an intranet could take ages and would constantly be messed with because being web designers they would want to keep changing the layout.

Advantages of Google Docs	Disadvatanges of Google Docs
Documents can be saved and accessed anywhere there is the internet	Need to have a compatible browser to view it on
No need for portable hardware devices (such as a USB)	Need internet access to access the documents
Only one document is used at any one time	Only small documents can be used at a time
Work can continue from anywhere in the world	Has less features that other software can provide (like Microsoft)
Has a simple easy to use interface	

This explanation of how the team could use Google Docs and why is it better than other methods covers M1.

The advantages and disadvantages table help to justify the choice of Google Docs.

Possible safety problems are explained.

Suggestion are made as to how to avoid possible problems.

Sample learner work: page 3

Is Google Docs safe to use (D1):

Most people say Google docs is secure, but as with anything in the internet it is as secure as it can be and that is down to the people you allow to share the documents and the protection and security you have on your own computer. At the moment there are no checks on Googles' behalf as to who the documents can be shared with.

If one computer has a virus that a member of staff is working on, he uploads the document to Google Docs and then that document is then downloaded onto another machine, the virus is then passed on. In a business situation this could be terrible because the websites that Inspiration are creating could contain viruses and then they pass them onto their clients, and the virus could then get passed on whenever the website is accessed.

I suppose the key is to use the facility wisely and don't upload anything that would be too valuable, like clients details and addresses, or company account details. From the communication point of view though for having general discussions, I see no harm and it keeps staff informed about what is going on in the company.

It will also mean the manager will have a better idea of the dynamic of the team and what they are all thinking. He may be able to recognise who's got which strengths and weaknesses and so he will be able to plan and move people round to do certain jobs to the companies advantage. This could be very beneficial from the company's productivity point of view.

If any of the information that was put on Google docs became inappropriate, the manager could delete the documents concerned and reprimand the employee that is involved. This would reflect poorly on the company and could mean that Google Docs may cancel the companies account and therefore taking away this method of communicating. But you would like to think in a professional environment this would not be an issue.

I would suggest the manager give this method of communication a try and if it doesn't work he could always schedule weekly meetings or invest in video conferencing resources that they can all use from their desks, that way they can all discuss and chat about work related stuff in a modern face to face fashion.

Sample assessor's comments

It's useful to add your own feedback on what you felt went well and what didn't go so well when completing the assignment. This may help you with future assignments and may also help your tutor to produce a better version of the assignment next year.

You need to make sure you complete at least all the pass criteria, otherwise you will fail the unit.

Qualification	BTEC Level 2 First Diploma in Information Technology	Assessor name	Anita Wainright
Unit number and title	Unit 1: Communicating in the IT Industry	Learner name	John Atkins

Grading criteria	Achieved?
P6 Explain the social impacts of the use of IT	Y
M2 Discuss the potential threats which the use of IT has introduced	Y

Learner feedback

I struggled a bit with the Publisher software, but once I got into it I was able to research the criteria. I enjoyed looking into the threats of an IT system and found it useful because I use my computer at home a lot and was unaware of some of the problems that we could also get by using the internet.

Assessor feedback

Well done John, you produced a good quality news article here. I can tell you worked hard on your layout and my only criticism is the font in the lower part of the article is smaller and a little difficult to read. Keep up the good work and you are well on your way to a distinction overall in this unit.

Action plan

In future tasks like this one, I think it would be good to look at your writing skills. We need to make sure you stay in the same tense, remember who your target audience is and remember to keep the theme of the article consistent throughout.

Assessor signature	Anita Wainright	Date	5 June 2011
Learner signature	John Atkins	Date	5 June 2011

Read the assessor feedback carefully as it will help you to identify what you did well and what you need to do to improve.

The action plan is particularly important as it tells you what you need to do to achieve any grades you have not passed.

Qualification	BTEC Level 2 First in Information Technology	Assessor name	Anita Wainright
Unit number and title	Unit 1: Communicating in the IT Industry	Learner name	John Atkins

Grading criteria	Achieved?
P5 Select, set up and use a specialist communication channel to communicate and exchange information	Y
M1 Justify why a specialist communication channel is effective for a given purpose	Y
D1 Explain how to ensure safe and secure use of a specialist communication channel	Y

Learner feedback

This was a really interesting task to do and made a change from the other tasks. I enjoyed working with my classmates and getting them to pretend to be someone else and although I found it difficult to motivate them to contribute to the forum for P5, it was worth the effort in the end. I was also pleased with the merit and distinction evidence because writing isn't my strong point and I needed some guidance in how to put my words across correctly in a proper grammatical way.

Assessor feedback

You have done really well on this task John, and despite your lack of confidence at the start, this is real progress for you. I found the discussion on the forum that you set up an interesting read and some people contributed some very valid points (evidenced on page 2). And despite your grammar and spelling issues you have produced a very well-structured report to finish and conclude the assignment.

Action plan

In future assignments I would suggest that you make sure you proofread all the work that you submit and if necessary use some of the techniques I showed you in class to help you achieve the higher grades. An excellent effort – well done.

Also, remember to reference any websites or books you used to help you answer the tasks. We will look at this together next time in class so you are aware for the next assignment.

Assessor signature	Anita Wainright	Date	5 June 2011
Learner signature	John Atkins	Date	5 June 2011

Your BTEC First course

Coping with problems

Most learners sail through their BTEC First with no major problems. Unfortunately, not everyone is so lucky. Some may have personal difficulties or other issues that disrupt their work so they are late handing in their assignments. If this happens to you, it's vital to know what to do. This checklist should help.

Checklist for coping with problems

✔ Check that you know who to talk to.

✔ Don't sit on a problem and worry about it. Talk to someone promptly, in confidence. It's always easier to cope if you've shared it with someone.

✔ Most centres have professional counsellors you can talk to if you prefer. They won't repeat anything you say to them without your permission.

✔ If you've done something wrong or silly, people will respect you more if you are honest, admit where you went wrong and apologise promptly.

Case study: Coping with problems

Suraj wants to give up the course. It is all too much. He is way behind with his work and is finding home life really difficult. He is having constant arguments with his stepfather and he really wants to leave home. He feels the situation is hopeless and he can't cope.

Suraj goes to see his class tutor to tell her that he is giving up. She asks him why and Suraj explains that he is late with three assignments and hasn't even started on the one due next week. His tutor wants to know why he has got so far behind after he had made such a good start on the course. Suraj explains about the problems with his stepfather and that he wants to leave home. He can't do college work at home and the worry and upset is distracting him.

His tutor explains that when learners have genuine problems like this it is usually possible to arrange an extension to assignment deadlines. She emails the tutors concerned, asking them if they could give Suraj extra time until the end of term to complete the outstanding work. She also puts him in touch with a learning advisor in the Learning

Resource Centre who will meet up with him each week to help him with his assignments. Finally, she contacts the college counsellor and arranges an interview for Suraj.

Suraj feels a bit better after seeing his tutor. At least the pressure of the missed assignment deadlines is off.

The following week he goes to see the counsellor and they have a long chat about his home situation. The counsellor explains how hard it can be to find accommodation away from home but she gives him details of an organisation that helps young people to find housing. They also talk about how to deal with the tension between him, his mother and his stepfather. The counsellor arranges a meeting with all three of them to discuss the issues and problems.

By the end of term, Suraj has completed all his outstanding work. The situation at home has improved a bit and, having spoken to the housing charity, he has decided to stay at home for the time being. In the end, he is glad he didn't give up the course.

What would you do if you were in a similar situation to Suraj's?

TOP TIP

If you have a serious complaint or concern, talk to your chosen tutor first – for example if you believe an assignment grade is unfair. All centres have official procedures to cover important issues such as appeals about assignments and formal complaints but it's usually sensible to try to resolve a problem informally first.

Activity: Knowing where to get help

There are lots of different places you can go to, and people you can speak to, that can help you deal with problems you may have during your course. Some of these are informal sources – like your friends and family – others are more formal sources provided by your school or college, and by Edexcel.

Use the table below to list the contact details of various people who may be able to help you with problems.

Source of help/information	Telephone number	Email address/website
Tutor/Head of Year		
School or college department office		
Careers advisor		
Youth worker/counsellor		
Edexcel		www.edexcel.co.uk
Student Union		www.nus.org.uk
Learning advisor		
Class representative		
Connexions		www.connexions-direct.com

Skills building

To do your best in your assignments you need a number of skills, including:
- your **personal, learning and thinking skills**
- your **functional skills** of ICT, mathematics and English
- your proofreading and document-production skills.

Personal, learning and thinking skills (PLTS)

These are the skills, personal qualities and behaviour that you find in people who are effective and confident at work. These people enjoy carrying out a wide range of tasks, always try to do their best and work well alone or with others. They enjoy a challenge and use new experiences to learn and develop.

Activity: How good are your PLTS?

1   Do this quiz to help you identify areas for improvement.

   a) I get on well with other people.

      Always   **Usually**   **Seldom**   **Never**

   b) I try to find out other people's suggestions for solving problems that puzzle me.

      Always   **Usually**   **Seldom**   **Never**

   c) I plan carefully to make sure I meet my deadlines.

      Always   **Usually**   **Seldom**   **Never**

   d) If someone is being difficult, I think carefully before making a response.

      Always   **Usually**   **Seldom**   **Never**

   e) I don't mind sharing my possessions or my time.

      Always   **Usually**   **Seldom**   **Never**

   f) I take account of other people's views and opinions.

      Always   **Usually**   **Seldom**   **Never**

   g) I enjoy thinking of new ways of doing things.

      Always   **Usually**   **Seldom**   **Never**

   h) I like creating new and different things.

      Always   **Usually**   **Seldom**   **Never**

   i) I enjoy planning and finding ways of solving problems.

      Always   **Usually**   **Seldom**   **Never**

j) I enjoy getting feedback about my performance.

    Always   **Usually**   **Seldom**   **Never**

k) I try to learn from constructive criticism so that I know what to improve.

    Always   **Usually**   **Seldom**   **Never**

l) I enjoy new challenges.

    Always   **Usually**   **Seldom**   **Never**

m) I am even-tempered.

    Always   **Usually**   **Seldom**   **Never**

n) I am happy to make changes when necessary.

    Always   **Usually**   **Seldom**   **Never**

o) I like helping other people.

    Always   **Usually**   **Seldom**   **Never**

Score 3 points for each time you answered 'Always', 2 points for 'Usually', 1 point for 'Seldom' and 0 points for 'Never'. The higher your score, the higher your personal, learning and thinking skills.

2 How creative are you? Test yourself with this activity. Identify 50 different objects you could fit into a matchbox at the same time! As a start, three suitable items are a postage stamp, a grain of rice, a staple. Can you find 47 more?

Functional skills

Functional skills are the practical skills you need to function confidently, effectively and independently at work, when studying and in everyday life. They focus on the following areas:

- Information and Communications Technology (ICT)
- Maths
- English.

You may already be familiar with functional skills. Your BTEC First tutors will give you more information about how you will continue to develop these skills on your new course.

ICT skills

These will relate directly to how much 'hands-on' practice you have had on IT equipment. You may be an experienced IT user and using word processing, spreadsheet and presentation software may be second nature. Searching for information online may be something you do every day – in between downloading music, buying or selling on eBay and updating your Facebook profile!

Or you may prefer to avoid computer contact as much as possible. If so, there are two things you need to do.

1   Use every opportunity to improve your ICT skills so that you can start to live in the 21st century!

2   Make life easier by improving your basic proofreading and document preparation skills.

Proofreading and document preparation skills

Being able to produce well-displayed work quickly will make your life a lot easier. On any course there will be at least one unit that requires you to use good document preparation skills.

Tips to improve your document production skills

✔ If your keyboarding skills are poor, ask if there is a workshop you can join. Or your library or resource centre may have software you can use.

✔ Check that you know the format of documents you have to produce for assignments. It can help to have a 'model' version of each type in your folder for quick reference.

✔ Practise checking your work by reading word by word – and remember not to rely on spellcheckers.

Activity: How good are your ICT skills?

1a)   Test your current ICT abilities by responding *honestly* to each of the following statements.

i)   I can create a copy of my timetable using a word-processing or spreadsheet package.
True   **False**

ii)   I can devise and design a budget for myself for the next three months using a spreadsheet package.
True   **False**

iii)   I can email a friend who has just got broadband to say how to minimise the danger of computer viruses, what a podcast is and also explain the restrictions on music downloads.
True   **False**

iv)   I can use presentation software to prepare a presentation containing four or five slides on a topic of my choice.
True   **False**

v)   I can research online to compare the performance and prices of laptop computers and prepare an information sheet using word-processing software.
True   **False**

vi)   I can prepare a poster, with graphics, for my mother's friend, who is starting her own business preparing children's party food, and attach it to an email to her for approval.
True   **False**

TRY THIS

Learning to touch type can save you hours of time. Go to page 90 to find out how to access a useful website where you can check your keyboarding skills.

TOP TIP

Print your work on good quality paper and keep it flat so that it looks good when you hand it in.

1b) Select any one of the above to which you answered false and learn how to do it.

2 Compare the two tables below. The first is an original document; the second is a typed copy. Are they identical? Highlight any differences you find and check them with the key on page 89.

Name	Date	Time	Room
Abbott	16 July	9.30 am	214
Grey	10 August	10.15 am	160
Johnston	12 August	2.20 pm	208
Waverley	18 July	3.15 pm	180
Jackson	30 September	11.15 am	209
Gregory	31 August	4.20 pm	320
Marshall	10 September	9.30 am	170
Bradley	16 September	2.20 pm	210

Name	Date	Time	Room
Abbott	26 July	9.30 am	214
Gray	10 August	10.15 am	160
Johnson	12 August	2.20 pm	208
Waverley	18 July	3.15 am	180
Jackson	31 September	11.15 am	209
Gregory	31 August	4.20 pm	320
Marshall	10 September	9.30 pm	170
Bradley	16 August	2.20 pm	201

Maths or numeracy skills

TOP TIP

Quickly test your answers. For example, if fuel costs 85p a litre and someone is buying 15 litres, estimate this at £1 x 15 (£15) and the answer should be just below this. So if your answer came out at £140, you'd know immediately that you'd done something wrong!

Four easy ways to improve your numeracy skills

1 Work out simple calculations in your head, like adding up the prices of items you are buying. Then check if you are correct when you pay for them.

2 Set yourself numeracy problems based on your everyday life. For example, if you are on a journey that takes 35 minutes and you leave home at 11.10am, what time will you arrive? If you are travelling at 40 miles an hour, how long will it take you to go 10 miles?

3 Treat yourself to a Maths Training program.

4 Check out online sites to improve your skills. Go to page 90 to find out how to access a useful website.

Activity: How good are your maths skills?

Answer as many of the following questions as you can in 15 minutes. Check your answers with the key on page 89.

1 **a)** 12 + 28 = ?

  i) 30   ii) 34   iii) 38   iv) 40   v) 48

b) 49 ÷ 7 = ?

  i) 6   ii) 7   iii) 8   iv) 9   v) 10

c) ½ + 1¼ = ?

  i) ¾   ii) 1½   iii) 1¾   iv) 2¼   v) 3

d) 4 × 12 = 8 × ?

  i) 5   ii) 6   iii) 7   iv) 8   v) 9

e) 16.5 + 25.25 – ? = 13.25

  i) 28.5   ii) 31.25   iii) 34.5   iv) 41.65   v) 44

2 **a)** You buy four items at £1.99, two at 98p and three at £1.75. You hand over a £20 note. How much change will you get? _____

b) What fraction of one litre is 250 ml? _____

c) What percentage of £50 is £2.50? _____

d) A designer travelling on business can claim 38.2p a mile in expenses. How much is she owed if she travels 625 miles? _____

e) You are flying to New York in December. New York is five hours behind British time and the flight lasts eight hours. If you leave at 11.15 am, what time will you arrive? _____

f) For your trip to the United States you need American dollars. You find that the exchange rate is $1.5 dollars.

  i) How many dollars will you receive if you exchange £500? _____

  ii) Last year your friend visited New York when the exchange rate was $1.8. She also exchanged £500. Did she receive more dollars than you or fewer – and by how much? _____

g) A security guard and his dog patrol the perimeter fence of a warehouse each evening. The building is 480 metres long and 300 metres wide and the fence is 80 metres out from the building on all sides. If the guard and his dog patrol the fence three times a night, how far will they walk? _____

English skills

Your English skills affect your ability to understand what you read, prepare a written document, say what you mean and understand other people. Even if you're doing a practical subject, there will always be times when you need to leave someone a note, tell them about a phone call, read or listen to instructions – or write a letter for a job application!

Six easy ways to improve your English skills

1   Read more. It increases the number of words you know and helps to make you familiar with correct spellings.

2   Look up words you don't understand in a dictionary and check their meaning. Then try to use them yourself to increase your vocabulary.

3   Do crosswords. These help increase your vocabulary and practise your spelling at the same time.

4   You can use websites to help you get to grips with English vocabulary, grammar and punctuation. Go to page 90 to find out how to access a useful website for this page.

5   Welcome opportunities to practise speaking in class, in discussion groups and during presentations – rather than avoiding them!

6   Test your ability to listen to someone else by seeing how much you can remember when they've finished speaking.

Activity: How good are your English skills?

1   In the table below are 'wrong' versions of words often spelled incorrectly. Write the correct spellings on the right. Check your list against the answers on page 89.

Incorrect spelling	Correct spelling
accomodation	
seperate	
definate	
payed	
desparate	
acceptible	
competant	
succesful	

2 Correct the error(s) in these sentences.

a) The plug on the computer is lose.

_____

b) The car was stationery outside the house.

_____

c) Their going on they're holidays tomorrow.

_____

d) The principle of the college is John Smith.

_____

e) We are all going accept Tom.

_____

3 Punctuate these sentences correctly.

a) Toms train was late on Monday and Tuesday.

_____

_____

b) She is going to France Belgium Spain and Italy in the summer.

_____

_____

c) He comes from Leeds and says its great there.

_____

_____

4 Read the article on copyright.

Copyright

Anyone who uses a photocopier can break copyright law if they carry out unrestricted photocopying of certain documents. This is because The Copyright, Designs and Patents Act 1988 protects the creator of an original work against having it copied without permission.

Legally, every time anyone writes a book, composes a song, makes a film or creates any other type of artistic work, this work is treated as their property (or copyright). If anyone else wishes to make use of it, they must get permission to do so and, on occasions, pay a fee.

Licences can be obtained to allow educational establishments to photocopy limited numbers of some publications. In addition, copies of an original document can be made for certain specific purposes. These include research and private study. Under the Act, too, if an article is summarised and quoted by anyone, then the author and title of the original work must be acknowledged.

   a) Test your ability to understand unfamiliar information by responding to the following statements with 'True' or 'False'.

     i) Students and tutors in schools and colleges can copy anything they want.
     True   False

     ii) The law which covers copyright is The Copyright, Designs and Patents Act 1988.
     True   False

     iii) A student photocopying a document in the library must have a licence.
     True   False

     iv) Copyright only relates to books in the library.
     True   False

     v) If you quote a newspaper report in an assignment, you don't need to state the source.
     True   False

     vii) Anyone is allowed to photocopy a page of a book for research purposes.
     True   False

   b) Make a list of key points in the article, then write a brief summary in your own words.

5 Nikki has read a newspaper report that a horse racing in the Kentucky Derby had to be put down. The filly collapsed and the vet couldn't save her. Nikki says it's the third time in two years a racehorse has had to be put down in the US. As a horse lover she is convinced racing should be banned in Britain and the US. She argues that fox hunting was banned to protect foxes, and that racehorses are more important and more expensive than foxes. Darren disagrees. He says the law is not working, hardly anyone has been prosecuted and fox hunting is going on just like before. Debbie says that animals aren't important whilst there is famine in the world.

   a) Do you think the three arguments are logical? See if you can spot the flaws and check your ideas with the suggestions on page 89.

   b) Sporting activities and support for sporting teams often provoke strong opinions. For a sport or team of your choice, identify two opposing views that might be held. Then decide how you would give a balanced view. Test your ideas with a friend or family member.

Answers

Skills building answers

ICT activities

2 Differences between the two tables are highlighted in bold.

Name	Date	Time	Room
Abbott	**16** July	9.30 am	214
Grey	10 August	10.15 am	160
Johnston	12 August	2.20 pm	208
Waverley	18 July	3.15 **pm**	180
Jackson	**30** September	11.15 am	209
Gregory	31 August	4.20 pm	320
Marshall	10 September	9.30 **am**	170
Bradley	16 **September**	2.20 pm	**210**

Maths/numeracy activities

1 **a)** iv, **b)** ii, **c)** iii, **d)** ii, **e)** i

2 **a)** £4.83, **b)** ¼, **c)** 5%, **d)** £238.75, **e)** 2.15 pm, **f) i)** $750 **ii)** $150 dollars more, **g)** 6.6 km.

English activities

1 Spellings: accommodation, separate, definite, paid, desperate, acceptable, competent, successful

2 Errors:
   a) The plug on the computer is <u>loose</u>.
   b) The car was <u>stationary</u> outside the house.
   c) <u>They're</u> going on <u>their</u> holidays tomorrow.
   d) The <u>principal</u> of the college is John Smith.
   e) We are all going <u>except</u> Tom.

3 Punctuation:
   a) Tom's train was late on Monday and Tuesday.
   b) She is going to France, Belgium, Spain and Italy in the summer.
   c) He comes from Leeds and says it's great there.

4 **a) i)** False, **ii)** True, **iii)** False, **iv)** False, **v)** False, **vi)** False, **vii)** True

5 A logical argument would be that if racehorses are frequently injured in a particular race, eg one with difficult jumps, then it should not be held. It is not logical to compare racehorses with foxes. The value of the animal is irrelevant if you are assessing cruelty. Darren's argument is entirely different and unrelated to Nikki's. Whether or not fox hunting legislation is effective or not has no bearing on the danger (or otherwise) to racehorses. Finally, famine is a separate issue altogether. You cannot logically 'rank' problems in the world to find a top one and ignore the others until this is solved!

Accessing website links

Links to various websites are referred to throughout this BTEC Level 2 First Study Skills Guide. In order to ensure that these links are up-to-date, that they work and that the sites aren't inadvertently linked to any material that could be considered offensive, we have made the links available on our website: www.pearsonhotlinks.co.uk. When you visit the site, search for either the title BTEC Level 2 first Study Skills Guide in IT or ISBN 9781846905704. From here you can gain access to the website links and information on how they can be used to help you with your studies.

Useful terms

Apprenticeships
Schemes that enable you to work and earn money at the same time as you gain further qualifications (an NVQ award and a technical certificate) and improve your functional skills. Apprentices learn work-based skills relevant to their job role and their chosen industry. See page 90 for how to access a useful website to find out more.

Assessment methods
Methods, such as practical tasks and assignments, which are used to check that your work demonstrates the learning and understanding you need to obtain the qualification.

Assessor
The tutor who marks or assesses your work.

Assignment
A complete task or mini-**project** set to meet specific grading criteria.

Assignment brief
The information and instructions related to a particular assignment.

BTEC Level 3 Nationals
Qualifications you can take when you have successfully achieved a Level 2 qualification, such as BTEC First. BTEC Level 3 Nationals are offered in a variety of subjects.

Credit value
The number of credits attached to your BTEC course. The credit value increases relative to the length of time you need to complete the course, from 15 credits for a BTEC Certificate, to 30 credits for a BTEC Extended Certificate and 60 credits for a BTEC Diploma.

Command word
The word in an assignment that tells you what you have to do to produce the type of answer that is required, eg 'list', 'describe', 'analyse'.

Educational Maintenance Award (EMA)
This is a means-tested award which provides eligible learners under 19, who are studying a full-time course at a centre, with a cash sum of money every week. See page 90 for how to access a useful website to find out more.

Functional skills
The practical skills that enable all learners to use and apply English, Maths and ICT both at work and in their everyday lives. They aren't compulsory to achieve on the course, but are of great use to you.

Grade
The rating of pass, merit or distinction that is given to an assignment you have completed, which identifies the standard you have achieved.

Grading criteria
The standard you have to demonstrate to obtain a particular grade in the unit. In other words, what you have to prove you can do.

Grading grid
The table in each unit of your BTEC qualification specification that sets out the grading criteria.

Indicative reading
Recommended books, magazines, journals and websites whose content is both suitable and relevant to the unit.

Induction
A short programme of events at the start of a course or work placement designed to give you essential information and introduce you to other people so that you can settle in easily.

Internal verification
The quality checks carried out by nominated tutors at all centres to ensure that all assignments are at the right level and cover appropriate learning outcomes. The checks also ensure that all **assessors** are marking work consistently and to the same standards.

Learning outcomes
The learning and skills you must demonstrate to show that you have learned a unit effectively.

Levels of study

The depth, breadth and complexity of knowledge, understanding and skills required to achieve a qualification determines its level. Level 2 is equivalent to GCSE level (grades A* to C). Level 3 equates to GCE A-level. As you successfully achieve one level, you can progress on to the next. BTEC qualifications are offered at Entry Level, then Levels 1, 2, 3, 4, 5, 6 and 7.

Mandatory units

On a BTEC Level 2 First course, these are the compulsory units that all learners must complete to gain the qualification.

Optional units

Units on your course from which you may be able to make a choice. They help you specialise your skills, knowledge and understanding and may help progression into work or further education.

Personal, learning and thinking skills (PLTS)

The skills and qualities that improve your ability to work independently and be more effective and confident at work. Opportunities for developing these are a feature of all BTEC First courses. They aren't compulsory to achieve on the course, but are of great use to you.

Plagiarism

Copying someone else's work or work from any other sources (eg the internet) and passing it off as your own. It is strictly forbidden on all courses.

Portfolio

A collection of work compiled by a learner – for an **assessor** – usually as evidence of learning.

Project

A comprehensive piece of work which normally involves original research and planning and investigation either by an individual or a team. The outcome will vary depending upon the type of project undertaken. For example, it may result in the organisation of a specific event, a demonstration of a skill, a presentation or a piece of writing.

Tutorial

An individual or small group meeting with your tutor at which you discuss the work you are currently doing and other more general course issues.

Unit content

Details about the topics covered by the unit and the knowledge and skills you need to complete it.

Work placement

Time spent on an employer's premises when you carry out work-based tasks as an employee and also learn about the enterprise to develop your skills and knowledge.

Work-related qualification

A qualification designed to help you to develop the knowledge and understanding you need for a particular area of work.